Entrepreneurship Development in Saitual Sericulture Cluster in Mizoram

Entrepreneurship Development in Saitual Sericulture Cluster in Mizoram

Dr. Lalzuitluangi

KALPAZ

ISBN: 978-93-5324-293-0

First Published, 2020

Published by

Kalpaz Publications
C-30, Satyawati Nagar,
Delhi – 110052
Ph.: 011-47034999, 9811692060
www.kalpazpublications.com
E-mail: kalpaz@hotmail.com

Printed at: G. Print Process, Delhi

Contents

Chapter - 1

Introduction

1. Introduction

Entrepreneurship is a necessary ingredient for stimulating economic growth and employment opportunities in all societies. Entrepreneurial activities differ substantially depending on the type of organization and creativity involved. It may pertain to agriculture, industry, trade or other professions. In the developing world, successful small businesses are the primary engines of job creation, income growth, and poverty reduction.

Clusters are sectoral and geographical concentration of enterprises, in particular Small and Medium Enterprises (SMEs), faced with common opportunities and threats which can give rise to external economies and favor the emergence of specialized technical, administrative and financial services. The industrial cluster is not a new economic phenomenon. Its genesis can be traced centuries earlier; however it emerged as a tool for developing micro, small and medium enterprises at the end of the 1990's with the success of numerous clusters in Italy.

In India, clusters development initiatives gathered momentum in 2000 and today cluster has emerged as a key strategy for regional and economic development for both developed and developing economies. In India, there are a number of industrial clusters which have evolved over a long period of time. Most of the clusters were established naturally as traditional activities of local communities (NCEUS, 2009). These include artisanal, traditional, and modern industries.

Sericulture is a largely village-based industry providing employment opportunities to a large section of the rural population in India. Sericulture, or silk farming, is the rearing of silkworms for the production of silk. It is an agro-based industry and has a very short gestation period, having the potential to generate adequate returns from even small areas of land.

Sericulture has the potential to provide gainful self-employment to farmer households in rural areas (Government of India, 2013).

2. A Conceptual Framework

2.1. Entrepreneurship

Entrepreneurship is the process of starting a business or other organization. Entrepreneurship comes from the term entrepreneur which is derived from the root French word 'entreprendre', which means, 'to undertake'. Cantillon(1755) considered an entrepreneur to be a risk taker who deliberately allocates resources to exploit opportunities in order to maximize the financial return and Say (1803) referred to an entrepreneur as an organizer.Schumpeter(1934) described entrepreneurs as innovators who change the status quo to set up new products and new services.

The term entrepreneur evolved different meanings in later years. Drucker (1985) defined an entrepreneur as one who always searches for change, responds to it and exploits it as an opportunity. According to Stevenson and Jarillo entrepreneurship is "a process by which individuals –either on their own or within organizations– pursue opportunities" where as Eckhardt and Shane define it as a business process which includes the identification and assessment of opportunities, the decision to exploit them oneself or sell them, efforts to obtain resources and the development of the strategy and organization of the new business project (as cited in Cuervo, Ribeiro and Salvador, 2005).

2.2. Agribusiness

Agribusiness is definedas *a*griculture conducted on commercial principles (Oxford Dictionary). Agricultural product shall include not only produce of agriculture but also horticulture, sericulture, animal husbandry, dairy husbandry, floriculture, fisheries, Apiculture and includes minor forest produce & live stock based products (Government of Karnataka, 2011).

Agro based industry includes units which add value to agricultural products/intermediates/residues, both food and non-food, by processing into products which are marketable or usable or edible, or by improving storability, or by providing the link from farm to the market or a part thereof. Agro based industry also includes dry land farming, precision farming, growing under controlled conditions, extensive IT and GIS application in agriculture &farming solutions, hi-tech cultivation, agri-input sectors, agriculture engineering sector, agri service sector and other such industrial

/ processing / manufacturing / service units pertaining to the agribusiness sector(Government of Karnataka, 2011).

2.3. Agripreneur

There is no single definition of the term "Agripreneur". However, an agripreneur may be referred to as someone who undertakes a variety of activities in agriculture on a commercial basis. An agripreneur is therefore a person who conducts agribusiness (Mittal, 2006).

2.4. Clusters

Cluster generally suggest connection and association of firms that are linked vertically and horizontally through their commonalities and complementariness in products, services, inputs, technologies, transportation, warehouse, and communication (Porter, 1998).

UNIDO (2001) defines clusters as "A sectoral and geographical concentrations of enterprises that produce and sell a range of related or complementary products and, thus, face common challenges and opportunities. These concentrations can give rise to external economies such as emergence of specialized suppliers of raw materials and components or growth of a pool of sector-specific skills and foster development of specialized services in technical, managerial and financial matters".

The National Bank for Agricultural and Rural Development (NABARD), Cluster Development Programme: "Micro enterprises and household units functioning on Self Help Group (SHG) mode and having a minimum of 50 beneficiaries up to a maximum of 200. In intensive clusters, the number of beneficiaries may go up to 500-700 and can even extend over a block or taluka" (MSME foundation, 2007).

For a developing country like India cluster based approach aims at rural economic development, community development (through upliftment of traditional skills and knowledge etc), pro-poor growth, market development etc. According to a report (MSME foundation 2007), India has around 6000 micro enterprise clusters. Another database of UNIDO shows that there are more than 4000 artisanal and about 363 non- artisanal clusters in India. The overall picture in India shows a numerical domination of rural traditional artisanal clusters that are likely to be dominated entirely by small enterprises.

These small artisanal clusters play an important role in regional economic development in India (Das R and Das Kumar, 2011).

2.5. Sericulture

Sericulture is the art of rearing silkworms for the production of cocoons, which are the raw materials for silk production. Sericulture, a cottage industry par excellence, is one of the most labour-intensive sectors of the economy. Silk production, including sericulture, is well known as a highly employment-oriented, low capital activity ideally suited to the conditions of a labour-abundant and agro-based economy like India.

Sericulture combines both agriculture and industry. Mulberry cultivation, silk worm rearing and cocoon production are agricultural activities whereas reeling, twisting, weaving and marketing are industrial activities. This enterprise starts in agriculture sector and ends in the industrial sector (Rani, 2006).

Manufacturing of silk fabrics can be classified into two parts. The first part consists of sericulture, which involves four important operations viz., cultivation of mulberry, production of layings, rearing of silkworm, disposal of cocoons. The second part includes reeling, twisting, dyeing, weaving, printing and finishing. Silk industry, therefore, consists of sericulture, post-cocoon technology (reeling), pre-weaving technology (twisting), dyeing, weaving and printing. The propensity of silk industry therefore depends upon the propensity of sericulture (Rathnam, Narasaiah and Murthy, 2013).

According to Central Silk Board (2018), Ministry of Textiles, Government of India "Sericulture is an agro-based industry. It involves rearing of silkworms for the production of raw silk, which is the yarn obtained out of cocoons spun by certain species of insects. The major activities of sericulture comprises of food-plant cultivation to feed the silkworms which spin silk cocoons and reeling the cocoons for unwinding the silk filament for value added benefits such as processing and weaving. Women constitute over 60 % of those employed in down-stream activities of sericulture in the country. This is possible because sericulture activities starting from mulberry garden management, leaf harvesting and silkworm rearing is more effectively taken up by the women folk. Even silk reeling industry including weaving is largely supported by them.

3. What is Sericulture?

3.1. Silk through the ages: A historical perspective

Silk production has a long history. Silk was discovered by Xilingji (Hsi-ling-chi), wife of China's 3rd Emperor, Huangdi (Hoang-Ti), in 2640 B.C. While making tea, Xilingji accidentally dropped a silkworm cocoon into a cup of hot water and found that the silk fiber could be loosened and unwound. Fibers from several cocoons could be twisted together to make a thread that was strong enough to be woven into cloth. Thereafter, Hsiling chi discovered not only the means of raising silk worms, but also the manners of reeling silk and of employing it to make garments. Later sericulture spread throughout China, and silk became a precious commodity, highly sought after by other countries. Demand for this exotic fabric eventually created the lucrative trade route, the historically famous Silk Road or Silk Route named after its most important commodity. This road helped in taking silk westward and bringing gold, silver and wool to the East. With the mulberry silk moth native to China, the Chinese had a monopoly on the world's silk production. (Singh, 2017)

After 1200 B.C. Chinese immigrants who had settled in Korea helped in the emergence of silk industry in Korea. During the third century B.C. Semiramus, a general of the army of Empress Singu-Kongo, invaded and conquered Korea. Among his prisoners were some Sericulturists whom he brought back to Japan. They helped in the establishment and growth of sericulture industry in Japan. Another story is that a Chinese princess married an Indian prince. She carried silkworm eggs/mulberry cocoons in her elaborate head dress.

She disclosed the secret of raising silkworms thus, silk production spread in India. In 550A.D. moth eggs and mulberry seeds were smuggled from China by two Nestorian monks, sent by Emperor Justinian-I and silk production began in Byzantium. The th technique of sericulture spread throughout the Mediterranean countries during the 7th century AD and then to Africa, Spain and Sicily. During latter part of the 19 century, modern machinery, improved techniques and intensive research helped the growth of sericulture industry in Japan. At present, Japan, China, Korea, Italy, Soviet Union, France, Brazil and India are the chief silk producing countries in the World. (Singh, 2017)

3.2. Typology of Silk

There are five major types of silk of commercial importance, obtained from different species of silkworms which in turn feed on a number of food plants. These are:

- Mulberry
- Oak Tasar & Tropical Tasar
- Muga
- Eri

Table 1.1: Typology of Silk

Common Name	Scientific Name	Origin
Mulberry Silkworm	*Bombyx mori*	China
Common Name	Scientific Name	Origin
Tropical Tasar Silkworm	*Antheraea mylitta*	India
Oak Tasar Silkworm	*Antheraea proylei*	India
Oak Tasar Silkworm	*Antheraea frithi*	India
Oak Tasar Silkworm	*Antheraea compta*	India
Oak Tasar Silkworm	*Antheraea pernyi*	China
Oak Tasar Silkworm	*Antheraea yamamai*	Japan
Muga Silkworm	*Antheraea assama*	India
Eri Silkworm	*Philosamia ricini*	India

Source: Central Silk Board

Retrieved from:http://csb.gov.in/silk-sericulture/silk/

Except mulberry, other non-mulberry varieties of silks are generally termed as vanya silks. India has the unique distinction of producing all these commercial varieties of silk. The different types of silk are explained as follows:

3.2.1 Mulberry – The insect producing mulberry silk is a domesticated variety of silkworms, which has been exploited for over 4000 years. All the strains reared at present belong to the species *Bombyx mori* that in believed to be derived from the original Mandarina silkworm, *Bombyx mandarina* Moore. China in the native place of this silk worm, but now it has been introduced in all the silk producing countries like Japan, India, Korea, Italy, France and Russia. The races of mulberry silk worm may be identified on the basis of geographical distribution as Japanese, Chinese, European or Indian origin; or as Uni-, Bi- or Multi-voltine depending upon the number of generations produced in a year under natural conditions; or as Tri-, Tetra- and Penta-moulters according to the number of moults that occur during larval growth; or as pure strain and hybrid variety according to genetic recombination. Cultivation of mulberry plants is called moriculture. There are over 20 species of mulberry, of which four are common: *Morus alba*, *M. indica*, *M. serrata* and *M latifolia* (Singh, 2017).

3.2.2 Tasar – Several species of *Antheraea* are exploited for production of wild silk known as tasar silk. These are *Antheraea mylitta, A. pernyi, A.yamamai, A.paphia and A.royeli. A. mylitta* and *A. paphia* are reared in central and north eastern parts of India. Many regional strains known by different local names are also found. Three types of voltinism, namely Uni-, Bi- and Multi-voltine are found in *A. mylitta* and *A. paphia*. These are reared on trees of *Terminalia tomentosa* (Vern. Asan), *Terminalia arjuna* (Vern. Arjun), *Shorea robusta* (Vern. Saal) and *Zizyphus jujuba* (Vern. Ber). Rearing of *A. pernyi* and *A. royeli* has been introduced recently in Manipur. These are reared on *Quercus* or Oak. *A. pernyi* and *A.yamamai* are the tasar silk worms of China and Japan respectively. These species feed on Quercus or Oak trees and are normally bivoltine. Cultivation of food plants is generally avoided, as tasar silkworms are wild in nature and need to be reared outdoors. However, modern sericulturists prefer to cultivate the food plants for better supervision (Singh, 2017).

3.2.3 Muga – Muga is an Assamese word which indicates the golden brown (amber) colour of the cocoon. The Muga silk worm, *Antheraea assama* is mainly confined to the Brahmaputra valley of Assam and foothills of East Garo hills of Meghalaya. Its distribution in the wild state, however, extends from western Himalaya to Nagaland, Cachar district of Assam and south Tripura. However, commercial exploitation is restricted only to north eastern India.

The Muga silk worm is multivoltne and passes through four moults and five instar stages. Generally 4-5 crops are raised in a year. Muga silkworm is a polyphagous insect. It feeds on the leaves of several kinds of trees, but *Machilus bombycine* (Vern. som) and *Litsaea polyantha* (Vern. soalu) are the two principal host food plants of muga silkworm. The host plants are cultivated through propagation by seeds or vegetatively by air layering. The plants are trained and pruned regularly (Singh, 2017).

3.2.4 Eri – The silk produced by *Philosamia ricini* is called Eri silk. The distribution of Eri silk worm is confined to Assam and bordering districts of West Bengal. The Eri silkworm is multivoltine and reared indoors 5-6 times a year. Optimum conditions required are 24-28°C temperature and 85-90% humidity. Adult moths emerge from morning to mid day; males emerge earlier than the females. After an hour of emergence mating occurs and continues till evening. Males are then separated. Eri worms are polyphagous having primary as well as secondary food plants (hosts). Primary food plants are *Ricinus communis* (Vern. Castor) and *Heteropenax fragrans* (Vern. Kasseru). Castor plants are of two varieties; the green leaved and violet leaved. Both are equally suitable for feeding the Eri silkworms. These plants are grown by seed sowing. Kasseru grows wild but may be cultivated as regular plantations on embankments around homestead land. It is grown by seed sowing and also vegetatively by stem cuttings. The secondary food plants are *Manihot utilissima* (Vern. Tapioca), *Evodia flaxinifola* (Vern. Payam), *Plumeria acutifolia* (Vern. Plum) and *Carica papaya* (Vern. Papaya)(Singh, 2017).

3.3 Life-cycle of Silkworm

The life cycle of silkworm consists of egg, larva, pupa (cocoon) and adult stages. Among these four stages, larval stage is the only feeding and active stage. The duration of larval period from hatching to spinning is about 26 days. During this long duration the larvae grow in size and enter cocoon (pupal) stage. To accommodate the larval body growth the larvae undergo four moults and thereby complete larval duration can be clearly differentiated into five instars or stadia. The first three instars (till the third moult) are known as young age or chawki and the last two instars are called as late age worms.

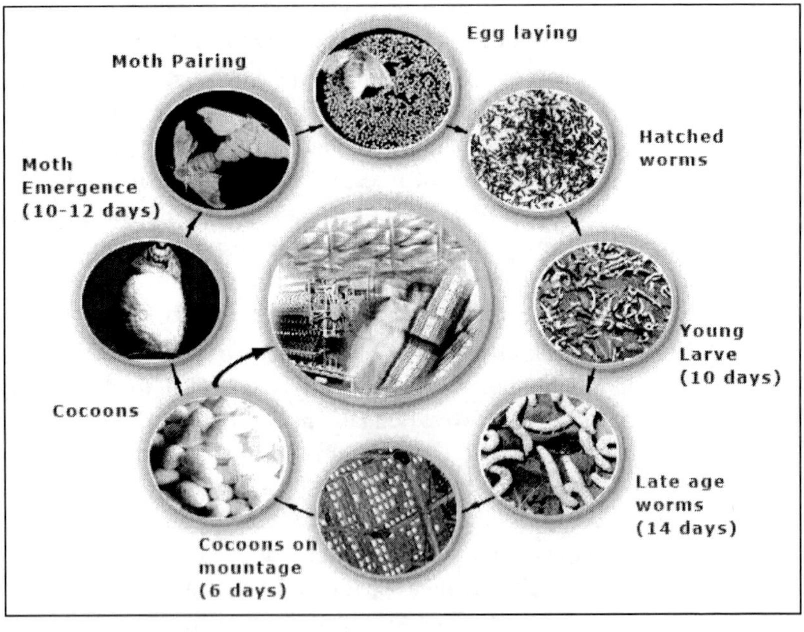

Source: Central Silk Board.
Retrieved from http://csb.gov.in/silk-sericulture/silk/life-cycle/

Figure 1: Life Cycle of Silkworm

3.4 Process of Sericulture

Sericulture is an art of rearing silkworm for the production of cocoons which is the raw material for the production of silk. It consists of four operations viz., Mulberry cultivation; Silk-worm egg (layings) production; Silkworm rearing and Disposal (marketing) of cocoons (Rathnam and Narasaiah, 2012).

(a) Plant/Mulberry cultivation – Normally mulberry plants are used for rearing silk worms. Mulberry cultivation is purely an agricultural operation and a major factor determining quantity of production and hence the profitability of sericulture. Mulberry plants yields leaf within six months after the saplings being planted under irrigated conditions.

(b) Silkworm egg Production- India has the unique distinction of being the only country producing all the five kinds of silkworms – Mulberry, Eri, Muga, Tropical Tasar and Temperate Tasar (Panday, Sharan and Mishra, 2005). The silkworm seed production centers are referred to as grainages. The silkworm seed known as Disease Free Layings are repaired in their centers and supplied to the farmers for rearing. Both Government and private sector grainages are involved in this activity.

(c) Silkworm Rearing – Silkworm rearing is a cottage activity carried by the sericulturists in their own house or in a separate shed built for this purpose. Silkworms are reared for the production of "cocoons" which is the raw material for silk production. The farmers rear silkworms and produce cocoons. By marketing the cocoons the farmers earn money. Silkworms are reared in well ventilated rearing shed following shoot rearing method.

(d) Disposal of Cocoons – Disposal of cocoons is minor activity but the sericulturist faces considerable difficulties in disposing of his cocoons. The disposal is bound by time factor as moths would emerge out of the cocoons after a certain time rendering the cocoons useless. The cocoons are sold at various government and private marketing yards and sometimes to middlemen and commission agents (Narasaiah, 2003).

After the successful completion of the process of Sericulture, the cocoon undergo the industrial process of reeling, spinning, weaving and utilization of silk waste and other by-products and finally the production of silk (Panday, Sharan and Mishra, 2005).

3.5 Indian Silk

Silk has been intermingled with the life and culture of the Indians. Though India is producing all the varieties of silk i.e., dress materials, scarves/ stoles, readymade garments, etc., the silk sarees are unique. The saree is almost synonymous with the word silk. It is the traditional costume of Indian woman since time immemorial. There are innumerable references in Indian literature about this draped garment and the style of wearing differs from time to time, region to region and people to people. The silk sarees of India are among the living examples of the excellent craftsmanship of the weavers of the country. The artistic and aesthetic sense of Indian weavers is not content with striking colours they choose for the fabrics, but lies in their mastery over the creation of floral designs, beautiful textures, fine geometry and the durability of such work. The weaver not only weaves with yarn but with intense feeling and emotion. In India, there are a number of silk weaving centers spread all over the country, known for their distinct and typical style and products. For Indians, particularly ladies, silk is lifeline - the elixir. Silk is always woven interwoven with way of life and culture of a region. Craftsmen all over the Indian sub-continent tried to master the weaving of sarees as exclusive as one can think of, putting motif designs, colours, pattern and versatility in them. No two sarees can be of same design left to the choice of weaver, thus there is innumerable pattern or diversity. Over the years, specific centres sprung and developed to promote a particular pattern of design / weaving and they became distinct. (Central Silk Board, 2018). Some of the famous silk centers in India are as under:-

Table 1.2: Famous Silk Centres in India

Sl. No.	*State*	*Silk Centre*
1.	Andhra	Dharmavaram, Narainpet Pochampalli, Venkatagiri,
2.	Assam	Sualkuchi
3.	Bihar	Bhagalpur
4.	Gujarat	Surat, Cambay
5.	Jammu & Kashmir	Srinagar
6.	Karnataka	Bangalore, Anekal, Ilkal, Molakalmuru, Melkote, Kollegal
7.	Chattisgarh	Champa, Chanderi, Raigarh
8.	Maharashtra	Paithan
9.	Tamil Nadu	Kanchipuram, Arni, Salem, Kumbhakonam, Tanjavur
10.	Uttar Pradesh	Varanasi
11.	West Bengal	Bishnupur, Murshidabad, Birbhum

Source: Central Silk Board

Retrieved from http://csb.gov.in/silk-sericulture/silks-of-india/

The Brocades of Banaras

Situated on the banks of the holy river Ganges, Varanasi is famous for its finest silk sarees and brocades. These sarees are known for rich and intricately woven motifs of leaf, flowers, fruits, birds, etc. on a soft colour background. They are enriched with intricate borders and heavily decorated pallus. The centre is also known for its gauzi silver and gold tissues, which are ultra-light in weight and delicate. The kinkab of Banaras is legendary. It is a glittering weave of gold and silver threads. The pure silk with a touch of gold is called bafta and the finely woven brocade of variegated silk is known as Amru (CSB, 2018)

The Patolas of Gujarat

The patolas are known for their precision subtlety and beauty. Here, both warp and weft are dyed by dye resist method in a range of five or six traditional colours like red, indigo, blue, emerald green, black or yellow. The exact and highly skilled process ensures that when the fabric is woven, the design will appear precisely and create a magnificently coloured and figured ground of great richness and beauty with birds, flowers, animals, dancers, etc. in a geometrically stylized perfection (CSB, 2018).

The Ballet of Bandhej

In bandhej or bandhini, the finely woven fabric is knotted tightly and dyed to achieve a distinct design. The sarees, odhnis (veils) and turbans of these regions are a medley of brilliant colours. The bandhini of Kutch is unmatched for their fineness of the minutely tied knots, the magnificence of the colours and the perfect designs (CSB, 2018).

The Tanchois of Gujarat

The tanchoi brocade was named after the three Parsi brothers called choi who learnt this art in China and introduced it to Surat. The choi brocade is usually a dark satin weave, purple or dark red in ground colour, embellished with motifs of flowers, creepers, birds all over design (CSB, 2018).

The Temple Silks of the South

South India is the leading silk producing area of the country also known for its famous silk weaving enclaves like Kancheepuram, Dharmavaram, Arni, etc. While the temple towns like Kancheepuram are renowned for their magnificent heavy silk sarees of bright colours with silver or gold zari works, the centers like Bangalore and Mysore are known for their excellent printed silks.

The traditional handloom silks always score over the powerloom silks in the richness of their textures and designs, in their individuality, character and classic beauty. Handloom weaving remains a symbol of versatility and creativity of living craft. Today, Indian silks, especially the handloom products, remain the most beautiful and cherished the world over (CSB, 2018).

4. Relevance of Silk to the Economy

Silk is a high value-added product and it always ranks comparably higher than any other textile fiber known in human history or in use in present times because of its appreciation in terms of consumer preference, unit values, fashion significance, employment generation, income generating opportunities in producer communities and the intangible value related to the preservation of mankind's cultural heritage. Over the centuries, silk has been recognized for its unique characteristics of comfort, luster and glamour. The most loved fiber, the world over, silk spells luxury, elegance and class with its unparalleled grandeur, the silk fabric has reigned as the undisputed "queen of textiles" over the centuries. The major silk producing countries in the world are; China, India, Uzbekistan, Brazil, Japan, Republic of Korea, Thailand, Vietnam, DPR Korea, Iran, etc.Few other countries are also engaged in the production of cocoons and raw silk in negligible quantities; Kenya, Botswana, Nigeria, Zambia, Zimbabwe, Bangladesh, Colombia, Egypt, Japan, Nepal, Bulgaria, Turkey, Uganda, Malaysia, Romania, Bolivia, etc. (Thiripura et al, 2018).

While the major producers are in Asia (90% of mulberry production and almost 100% of non-mulberry silk), sericulture industries have been lately established in Brazil, Bulgaria, Egypt and Madagascar as well. Sericulture is labour-intensive. About 1 million workers are employed in the silk sector in China. Silk Industry provides employment to 7.9 million people in India, and 20,000 weaving families in Thailand. China is the world's single biggest producer and chief supplier of silk to the world markets (Thiripura et al, 2018)

4.1. Global Silk Production

Table 1.3 shows the raw silk production of various countries across the globe for a period of 10 years from 2006-07 to 2015-16. The countries are

Table 1.3: Raw Silk Production in Various Countries (MT)

Year	*China*	*India*	*Brazil*	*Uzbekistan*	*Thailand*	*Vietnam*	*Korea republic*	*Japan*	*Bangladesh*	*Bulgaria*
2006-07	130000	18475	1387	950	1080	750	150	150	38	6.5
2007-08	108420	18320	1220	950	760	750	150	150	39	7.5
2008-09	98620	18370	1177	865	1100	680	135	95	39.50	7.5
2009-10	104000	19690	811	750	665	550	135	90	40	6.3
2010-11	115000	20410	770	940	655	550	300	54	40	9.4
2011-12	104000	23060	558	940	655	500	300	42	38	6
2012-13	126000	23679	614	940	655	450	300	30	42.50	8.5
2013-14	130000	26480	550	980	680	475	300	30	43	8.5
2014-15	146000	28708	560	1100	692	420	320	30	44.5	8
2015-16	170000	28523	600	1200	698	450	350	30	44	8

Source: Ministry of Textiles, www.texmin.nic.in

China, India, Brazil, Uzbekistan, Thailand, Vietnam DPR Korea, Japan, Bangladesh and Bulgaria.

It is evident from Table 1.3 that China is largest producer of raw silk during the period of 10 years followed by India and Brazil. As shown in the table the Raw silk production in China has increased from 130000 MT in 2006-07 to 170000 MT in 2015-16. The Raw silk production in India has increased from 18475 MT in 2006-07 to 28523 MT in 201516. However, it was found that the Raw silk production in Brazil has decreased from 1387MT in 2006-07 to 600 MT in 2015-16.

4.2. Silk Production in India

The silk industry originated in China, as early as 2640 BC according to tradition. Towards the 3rd century AD, knowledge of the silkworm and its product reached Japan through Korea; it probably spread to India a little later. India is the largest consumer of silk in the world. Silk is a unique fabric which has gradually crept in everybody's home in some way or the other. The Indian silk industry is an integral part of the Indian textile industry and is among the oldest industries in India. It engages around 60 lakh workers and it involves small and marginal farmers. Mulberry, Tasar, Muga and Eri are the types of silk produced in the Indian silk industry. Indian silk industry is the second highest contribution of silk to the world production. Consistent market demand and remarkable approach has led to the widening of this industry (Bhushi and Pharsiyawar, 2004). Silk is mainly produced in Pochampally, Kanchipuram, Dharmavaram, Mysore, etc., in South India and Banaras in the North for manufacturing garments and sarees. "Murshidabad silk", famous from historical times, is mainly produced in Malda and Murshidabad districts of West Bengal and woven with hand looms in Birbhum and Murshidabad districts. Another place famous for production of silk is Bhagalpur. The silk from Pochampally is particularly well known for its classic designs and enduring quality. The silk is traditionally hand-woven and handdyed and also usually has silver threads woven into the cloth (Sastry, 1984). Sericulture can help keeping the rural population employed and to prevent migration to big cities and securing remunerative employment; it requires small investments while providing raw material for textile industries (Thiripura et al, 2018)

Table 1.4 shows the Raw Silk Production of India for a period of 18 years from 2000-01 to 2017-18. It is clear that the raw silk production in India is showing an increasing trend with a total production of 15,857 MT in 2001-01 to 31,906 MT in 2017-18. Among the four varieties of silk

Table 1.4: Raw Silk Production in India (MT)

MULBERRY AND VANYA RAW SILK PRODUCTION STATISTICS (Unit: Metric Tonnes)					
Years	Mulberry	Tasar	Eri	Muga	Total
2000-01	14,432	237	1,089	99	15,857
2001-02	15,842	249	1,160	100	17,351
2002-03	14,617	284	1,316	102	16,319
2003-04	13,970	315	1,352	105	15,742
2004-05	14,620	322	1,448	110	16,500
2005-06	15,445	308	1,442	110	17,305
2006-07	16,525	350	1,485	115	18,475
2007-08	16,245	428	1,530	117	18,320
2008-09	15,610	603	2,038	119	18,370
2009-10	16,322	803	2,460	105	19,690
2010-11	16,360	1,166	2,760	124	20,410
2011-12	18,272	1,590	3,072	126	23,060
2012-13	18,715	1,729	3,116	119	23,679
2013-14	19,476	2,619	4,237	148	26,480
2014-15	21,390	2,434	4,726	158	28,708
2015-16	20,478	2,819	5,060	166	28,523
2016-17	21,273	3,268	5,637	170	30,348
2017-18	22,066	2,988	6,661	192	31,906

Source: Central Silk Board, Bengaluru

produced in India Mulberry has the largest production with 22,066 MT in 2017-018 followed by Tasar, Eri and then Muga.

4.2.1 State wise Raw Silk Prodcution

Table 1.5 shows the State-wise Raw Silk Production of India during the year 2015-16 to 2018-19. It is evident that over the years Karnataka is the largest producer of Raw Silk in India with a total production of 11592 MT in 2018-19. Andhra Pradesh is the second largest producer of raw silk with a total production of 7481 MT in 2018-19. Some of the other leading producers of raw silk in India include Telangana, Tamil Nadu, Kerala and

Maharashtra. Among the seven sisters of North-east India viz., Arunachal Pradesh, Assam, Meghalaya, Manipur, Mizoram, Nagaland and \, Assam is the leading producer of silk with 5029 MT in 2018-19. Mizoram is one of the leading producers among the North-east state with total production of 92 MT in 2018-19. The production of raw silk in Mizoram is showing an increasing trend from 64 MT in 2015-16 to 92 MT in 2018-19.

Table 1.5: State wise Raw Silk Production in India from 2015-16 to 2018-19 (in MT)

#	State	2015-16		2016-17		2017-18		2018-19	
		Target	Achmnt.	Target	Achmnt.	Target	Achmnt.	Target	Achmnt. (P)
1	Karnataka	10000	9823	11000	9571	11120	9322	10750	11592
2	Andhra Pradesh	6700	5086	5505	5970	6090	6778	7805	7481
3	Telangana	135	116	150	119	160	163	200	224
4	Tamil Nadu	1700	1898	2000	1914	2000	1984	2190	2072
5	Kerala	8	11	10	11	12	15	14	19
6	Maharashtra	248	274	285	259	328	373	415	519
7	Uttar Pradesh	265	256	280	269	300	292	340	289
8	Madhya Pradesh	207	257	275	111	230	103	160	83
9	Chhattisgarh	236	263	290	361	405	532	670	358
10	West Bengal	2601	2391	2706	2565	2590	2577	2775	2394
11	Bihar	61	67	84	77	85	63	95	53
12	Jharkhand	2207	2284	2622	2631	2744	2220	2658	2375
13	Odisha	118	117	130	125	140	116	148	129
14	Jammu & Kashmir	170	127	170	145	180	132	190	118
15	Himachal Pradesh	36	32	40	32	40	32	43	34
16	Uttarakhand	37	30	35	34	44	35	45	36
17	Haryana	1	0.6	1	1	2	0.7	2	0.7
18	Punjab	6	0.8	1	3	6	3	5	3
19	Assam & Bodoland	3330	3325	4103	3811	4705	4861	4980	5029
20	Ar.Pradesh	37	37	48	45	58	54	65	59
21	Manipur	428	519	530	529	560	388	435	464
22	Meghalaya	690	857	900	927	1070	1076	1110	1115
23	Mizoram	65	64	70	76	100	83.6	105	92
24	Nagaland	652	631	690	678	770	615	633	620
25	Sikkim	13	6	10	9	17	0.001	3	0.4
26	Tripura	51	52	65	75	85	87	125	102
Total		**30,000**	**28,523**	**32,000**	**30,348**	**33,840**	**31,906**	**35960**	**35,261**

Source: Central Silk Board

4.2.2 Silk Imports

While India exported small to moderate quantity of silk, imports have become a regular feature. The growth rates of silk imports showed an increasing trend. The import of silk goods in quantity terms increased at a compound growth rate of 9.82 percent per annum with instability of 31.96 percent, while the value registered a compound growth rate of 14.83 percent with instability of 44.23 percent during the study period. In the pre-WTO period, silk imports in quantity terms have increased at a compound growth rate of 13.69 percent and 30.12 percent in value terms. Similarly during post-WTO period, imports have increased at a compound growth rate of 15.10 percent in quantity and 8.90 percent in value. The main reason for this could be stagnant production of silk in the country. Moreover, weavers prefer imported raw silk as it is cheaper and also has good quality. And also increase in the domestic demand due to change in preferences of consumer to various value added silk products (Umesh K.B et al, 2009). The quantity and value of raw silk imported during 2015-16 to 2018-19 are given below:

Table 1.6: Raw Silk Imports

Year	*Quantity (MT)*	*Value (Rs. in Crores)*
2015-16	3529	1006.16
2016-17	3795	1092.26
2017-18	3712	1218.14
2018-19 (P)	2785	1041.40

4.2.3 Silk Exports

The silk goods export earnings have decreased over the years due to global recession and reduction in demand for silk goods in western countries (Western Europe and the USA, which are the major consumers of silk goods). However, the silk exports are picking up to the non-traditional/new markets such as the UAE, Nigeria, Sudan, Thailand etc., which is an encouraging sign. The export earnings during 2017-18 were Rs. 1,649.48 crores (CSB, 2019). Export values of silk goods during 2015-16 to 2018-19 are given below:

Table 1.7: Silk Exports

(Rs. in Crores)

Items	*2015-16*	*2016-17*	*2017-18*	*2018-19(P)*
Natural Silk Yarn	30.31	15.33	15.67	9.04
Silk Fabrics	1280.60	1051.65	864.81	396.39
Readymade Garments	1048.39	864.33	650.48	1184.54
Silk Carpet	16.88	63.78	17.34	113.09
Silk Waste	89.80	98.33	101.19	129.39
Total	2495.98	2093.42	1649.48	1832.45

Source: Compiled from the Statistics of DGCIS, Kolkata; P. Provisional.

5. Sericulture In North East India

The vegetation of Northeastern region is unique being characterized as one of the richest flora in the world, which produces a variety of products.

Northeastern India has the highest number of endemic plants, animal and microbial species. Many sericigenous insects along with their food plants are endemic to this region. Sericulture and weaving are part of the cultural heritage of the Northeastern region and is one of the most promising income sources to this region without spending much for its cultivation. The climate of North-east India is suitable for growth of non-mulberry silkworms, i.e. muga and eri (Unni et al, 2009).

Table 1.8: Distribution of Raw Silk in North-East India during 1980-81 to 2005-06

Year	Silk Variety	Assam Raw Silk (MT)	Meghalaya Raw Silk (MT)	Manipur Raw Silk (MT)	Mizoram Raw Silk (MT)	Nagaland Raw Silk (MT)	Tripura Raw Silk (MT)	Raw Silk (MT)
1980-81	Mulberry	7	NEG	05	NEG	02	NA	NA
	Muga	48	NA	NA	NA	NA	NA	NA
	Eri	95	34	NA	NA	NA	NA	NA
	Oak Tasar	NA	NA	NA	NA	NA	NA	NA
1985-86	Mulberry	15	0.37	23	0.4	0.45	0.24	NEG
	Muga	52	NA	NA	NA	NA	NA	NEG
	Eri	226	69	23	NA	09	NA	01
	Oak Tasar	NA	NA	NA	NA	NA	NA	NA
1990-91	Mulberry	13	01	23	0.4	01	02	01
	Muga	69	NA	NA	NA	NEG	NA	0.05
	Eri	335	115	189	NA	21	NA	05
	Oak Tasar	NA	NA	0.5	NA	0.35	NA	NA
1995-96	Mulberry	23	01	45	01	01	01	01
	Muga	86	0.8	0.52	NA	0.92	NA	0.1
	Eri	418	130	140	NA	18	NA	10
	Oak Tasar	0.01	NA	0.52	NA	NA	NA	NEG
2000-01	Mulberry	16.89	1.45	56.5	20.7	0.36	3.6	6.15
	Muga	94.32	13.85	0.111	NA	0.07	NA	0.334
	Eri	432	110	163	NA	26.1	NA	0.389
	Oak Tasar	NA	NA	0.054	0.08	NA	NA	0.10
2005-06	Mulberry	8.00	3.00	48	6.00	1.00	4.00	1.00
	Muga	104	5.40	0.06	0.07	0.18	NA	0.24
	Eri	745.00	280.00	235.00	3.20	130.00	NA	10.00
	Oak Tasar	NA	NA	3.00	NA	NEG	NA	NA

Source: Office of the Directorate (North Eastern Region), Central Silk Board, Guwahati, Assam

Notes: (i) NA means Not Available

(ii) NEG indicates production is less than 50 kilograms.

Table 1.8 shows the distribution of Raw-silk in North-East India during 1980-81 to 2005-16. It can been observed that during this period Assam is the leading producer of raw silk among the north-east states.

North East being a non-traditional area for Sericulture, Govt .of India has given special emphasis for consolidation and expansion of Sericulture in all the North Eastern States with critical interventions from host plantation development to finished products with value addition at every stage of production chain. As a part of this, under NERTPS - an Umbrella scheme of Ministry of Textiles, the Govt. of India have approved 38 Sericulture projects in all North Eastern States in the identified potential districts under three broadcategories viz., Integrated Sericulture Development Project (ISDP), Intensive Bivoltine Sericulture Development Project (IBSDP) and Aspirational Districts. A total of 38 projects covering Mulberry, Eri and Muga silk are implemented in all NE States. Total cost of these projects is Rs. 1,106.97 crore, of which GoI share is Rs. 955.07 crore. Objective of these projects is to establish sericulture as viable commercial activity in NER by creating necessary infrastructure and imparting skills to the locals for silkworm rearing and allied activities in the value chain. The projects are proposed to bring around 38,170 acres of plantation under mulberry, Eri and Muga sectors and expected to contribute additional production of 2,650 MT raw silk during the project period andgenerate employment for 3,16,000 persons. Under Integrated Sericulture Development Project (ISDP) sixteen projects have been approved with a total cost of Rs. 586.17 crore (GoI share of Rs. 483.35 crores) for implementation in Assam including BTC, Arunachal Pradesh, Manipur, Meghalaya, Mizoram, Nagaland and Tripura. The projects will support 27,010 acres plantation of Mulberry, Eri & Muga. This includes setting up of Silk Printing & Processing unit for Tripura, Soil to Silk for BTC (Assam) and Post Cocoon Technology for Nagaland. While 15 projects are meant for implementation by the State Sericulture Departments, one project - Creation of Seed Infrastructure is implemented by CSB to produce and ensure uninterrupted supply of quality seed to NE States. Till March-2019, Ministry has released Rs. 418.54 crore for the above projects, against which the expenditure reported is Rs. 359.73 crore (86%). (CSB, 2019)

6. Sericulture In Mizoram

Sericulture has been an agro industrial avocation and source of livelihood for the tribal people of Mizoram (Choudhury et al.2017).The state of Mizoram is endowed with a very pleasant and conducive climatic condition for silk worm rearing along with fertile soil and abundant rainfall giving a favourable atmosphere for excessive sericultural activities (Choudhury et al., 2013). Mulberry is cultivated in 5000 acres with 176 nos. of villages and occupies second place in producing Mulberry raw silk (54.92 MT) among the north eastern states (Annual report, CSB, 2015-16).

Mizoram is one of the states of Northeast India, with Aizawl as its capital. Mizoram's population is 1,091,014, according to 2011 census. It is the second least populous statein the country. Mizoram covers an area of approximately 21,087 square kilometers. About 95 percent of current Mizoram population is of diverse tribal origins who settled in the state. The literacy rate of Mizoram in 2011 was 91.33 percent. Mizoram has remained industrially backward (Directorate of Economics and Statistics, 2012).

Agriculture is the primary economic activity of the people of Mizoram. About 60 percent of the population depends upon agriculture and allied sector. Rice, corn (maize), cotton, and vegetables are the main crops cultivated. The government of Mizoram has assisted and encouraged an array of small-scale industries at the village level. Such industries include sericulture(silk production), handloom and handicrafts workshops, sawmills and furniture manufacturing, oil refining, grain milling, and ginger processing.

Sericulture remains one of the state's key industries. Sericulture was introduced in Mizoram way back in 1934 mainly as a source of livelihood and for the self-employment for the rural people of the state. Over the years sericulture is playing a vital role in uplifting the rural economy of Mizoram, as it has a potential to provide employment to the rural population of the state.

There is a vast potential for the development of sericulture in Mizoram. The climatic condition, fertility of the soil, rainfall etc. are most suitable for breeding of all kinds of silkworm. Interestingly, in Mizoram, all varieties of silk namely Mulberry, Eri, Muga and Tasar are commercially reared, mulberry being the most predominant. The state has made major advances in sericulture during the last decade and now provides subsidiary income to around 7826 families. The area covered under sericulture plantation is presently estimated to be 5826 hectares and it is recorded that sericulture activities is being pursued in 314 villages (Government of Mizoram, 2014).

In pursuance of the suggestion from the Planning Commission and Ministry of Textiles, Government of India, Central Silk Board (CSB) and Departments of Sericulture (DOS) of selected states has initiated Cluster Promotion Programme during 2007-12. The CBS and DOS have jointly identified 45 model sericulture clusters in pre-cocoon sector during 2008-09 and 2009-10, in 16 States including Mizoram. The sericulture department of Mizoram has selected 10 clusters under the 'Cluster area development project' namely Khamrang, Saitual, Darlung, Kanghmun, Khawhai,

Serchhip, Zobawk, Rotlang, Bawktlang and Lungbun as on 2011-12 (Directorate of Sericulture, Government of Mizoram, 2012).

Over the years sericulture is playing a vital role in development of the rural economy of Mizoram, in terms of employment opportunities. Mizoram occupies the 17th place in respect of area under mulberry, cocoon and silk raw production in India during 2011-2012 (Rathnam, Narasaiah and Murthy, 2013). The total area under mulberry and the total cocoon production was 2170 and 1650 hectares respectively and raw silk production during the period was 24 metric tonnes. Presently 12,000 farmers are practicing sericulture as an occupation in Mizoram (Directorate of Sericulture, 2012). A few years ago sericulture was considered a subsidiary occupation of farmers with small ownership. Now it is no longer a subsidiary occupation and more farmers are taking it up as an occupation.

Mizoram belongs to the non-traditional states which are practicing sericulture along with Andhra Pradesh, Assam, Bihar, Chhattisgarh, Madhya Pradesh, Himachal Pradesh, Manipur, Maharashtra and Uttarkhand etc. The traditional states are those states, which are practicing sericulture from ancient times while as non-traditional have adopted this practice recent times.

The contribution of non-traditional states in total mulberry raw silk production in India is 3.51% during 2012-13 and the share in total mulberry cultivation is about 17%. Maharashtra (0.90%) and then Madhya Pradesh (0.60%) Manipur (0.61%), Mizoram (0.15%) are the leading contributing states to total raw silk production in India (Table 2). As far as contribution among non-traditional states is concerned, the above story repeats as Maharashtra (25.79%) and then Madhya Pradesh 14.71%) Manipur (17.45%), Mizoram (4.55%) are the leading producers and rest contribution states is shown in Table 1.9 and Fig. 2 (Bhat, 2014).

Saitual is located in the Aizawl district of Mizoram. The Distance between Saitual and Aizawlis 77 km. According to the Census of India (2011), Saitual had a population of 11315, the male population being 5593 and that of female being 5722 and the total number of households is 1522. Saitual enjoys a moderate and pleasant climate. The economy of Saitual is basically agrarian in nature and the major agricultural crops grown are corn, sugarcane and vegetables. Sericulture has become an important occupation in recent years after the cluster started taking its shape in 2009. As mentioned earlier, Saitual has been identified as one among 10 sericulture clusters in Mizoram.

Table 1.9: Percentage share of Non-Traditional states in Mulberry Cultivation and Raw Silk Production in India

State	*% Share in Mulberry Raw silk during 2005-06*	*% share of Mulberry Raw Silk during 2012-13*	*% Share of Mulberry Raw Silk Production in Non-Traditional States in 2012-13*	*% share Under Mulberry Cultivation 2005-06*	*% share Under Mulberry Cultivation 2012-13*	*% Share of Mulberry Cultivation in Non-Traditional States in 2012-13*
Arunachal Pradesh	0.006	0.01	0.30	0.13	0.79	0.79
Assam	0.05	0.09	2.73	2.52	3.87	23.87
Bihar	0.019	0.06	1.97	0.22	0.32	1.98
Chhattisgarh	0.019	0.03	0.91	0.25	0.38	2.35
Himachal Pradesh	0.103	0.13	3.79	0.8	0.67	4.17
Jharkhand	0.006	0.01	0.30	0.04	0.10	0.67
Kerala	0.077	0.01	0.30	0.63	0.02	0.16
Madhya Pradesh	0.148	0.51	14.71	0.93	1.07	6.64
Maharashtra	0.284	0.90	25.79	0.79	0.94	5.79
Manipur	0.881	0.61	17.45	3.07	3.44	21.20
Meghalaya	0.019	0.05	1.66	0.56	1.00	6.15
Mizoram	0.038	0.15	4.55	2.26	1.25	7.71
Nagaland	0.006	0.02	0.60	0.2	0.29	1.83
Orissa	0.012	0.01	0.45	0.22	0.25	1.54
Punjab	0.025	0.01	0.30	0.35	0.45	2.80
Sikkim	0	0.01	0	0.07	0.10	0.80
Tripura	0.025	0.07	0.30	0.45	0.87	0.63
Uttarkhand	0.09	0.12	2.27	0.48	0.88	5.39
Sub Total (B)	1.39	3.51	3.49	11.43	17.10	5.43
Total A+B	100.00	100.00	100.00			

Source: Central Silk Board.

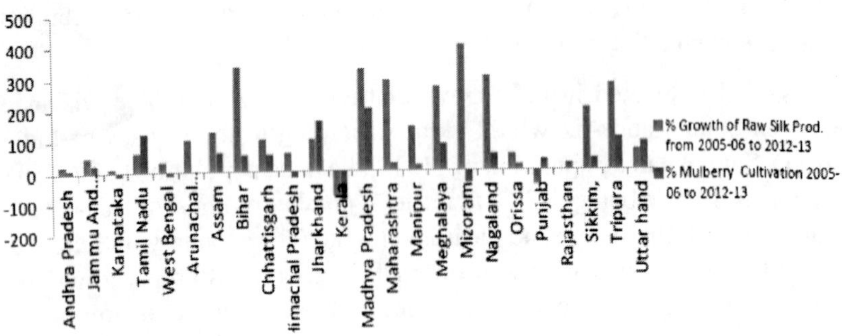

Source: Central Silk Board.

Figure 2: Percentage growth of raw silk production and mulberry cultivation.

6.1. Saitual Sericulture Cluster

The researcher found that about 180 households had undertaken sericulture activities on a commercial basis in Saitual. It is observed that two types of silkworm are mainly produced namely – the Mulberry silkworm and the Muga silkworm. The cluster is an ideal place for taking up sericulture activities with vast tracts of land under cultivation of mulberry leaves. In 2012, the sericulture department opened a Cocoon Purchasing Centre which consists of two cocoon drying machines. The government took the initiative to open this centre to further promote the sericulture activity in the cluster keeping in view the significant growth of sericulture in the cluster over the years and also recognizing the potential for further growth. Saitual has emerged as the cluster with the highest cocoon production in Aizawl district (Sericulture Department, Mizoram).

7. Cluster Development in Sericulture

7.1. What is a Cluster?

Broadly clusters may be defined as sectoral and geographical concentration of enterprises, in particular Small and Medium Enterprises (SME), faced with common opportunities and threats which can give rise to external economies and favour the emergence of specialised technical, administrative and financial services. Clusters have been defined and conceptualised differently by different scholars and practitioners.

Rosenfeld (1997) defined clusters as "Geographically bounded concentration of similar, related or complementary businesses with active channels for business transactions, communications and dialogue that share specialised infrastructure, labour markets and services, and that are faced with common opportunities and threats."

The UNIDO defined clusters as "A sectoral and geographical concentration of enterprises faced with common opportunities and threats which: (a) gives rise to external economies (e.g. specialised suppliers of raw materials, components and machinery, sector specific skills, etc, (b) favours the emergence of specialised infrastructures and services and (c) enables cooperation among public and private local institutions to promote local production, innovation and collective learning."

Porter (1998) defined clusters as "A geographically proximate group of interconnected companies and associated institutions in a particular field linked by commonalities and complementarities. Clusters encompass an array of linked industries and other entities important to competition, including governmental and other institutions - such as universities, standard setting agencies, think tanks, vocational training providers and trade associations."

According to the Organisation for Economic Cooperation and Development (OECD) "Clusters can be characterized as being networks of production of strongly interdependent firms (including specialised suppliers), knowledge producing agents (universities, research institutes, engineering companies), bridging institutions (brokers, consultants) and customers, linked to each other in a value adding production chain. The cluster approach focuses on the linkages and interdependence between actors in the network of production when producing products and services and creating innovations (Foundation for MSME, 2007).

Further, several agencies in India have defined clusters, on the basis of typology of clusters, their geographic range and minimum number of units. Some of these definitions are given hereunder:

The National Bank for Agricultural and Rural Development (NABARD), Cluster Development Programme: "Micro enterprises and household units functioning on Self Help Group (SHG) mode and having a minimum of 50 beneficiaries up to a maximum of 200. In intensive clusters, the number of beneficiaries may go up to 500-700 and can even extend over a block or *taluka*" (foundation for MSME, 2007).

The Government of Gujarat defined a cluster as follows: "A minimum of 50 industrial units, indulging in the manufacture of the same or related products and located within a radius of 10 kms in a particular location (Foundation for MSME, 2007)."

The Integrated Handloom Cluster Development Programme (IHCDP), Ministry of Textiles, Government of India defined a handloom cluster as one "having a minimum of 500 looms."

*The Development Commissioner (Handicrafts), Ministry of Textiles, Government of India*defined a handloom cluster as"Agglomerations having 100 artisans. In case of NER, Jammu & Kashmir and other hilly terrains, the clusters will have a minimum of 50 artisans (foundation for MSME, 2007)."

It is thus observed that there is no unanimity among the experts, policy makers and agencies about the meaning of clusters. However, a cluster should fulfill certain basic conditions such as: (a) the product range should not too wide and (b) the area covered provides scope for interaction among stakeholders.

7.2 Relevance of Clusters

Research evidence shows that clusters stimulate industrial growth and increase productivity. Many studies confirm the benefits of clustering for SMEs operating in the same or related industrial sectors (OECD, 2007) in both developed and developing countries.

Further, there are numerous examples that indicate that collective action by clustered firms has not only led to the improvement in product quality but also helped them in having access to larger markets (Schmitz, 1995 and World Development Report, 1995). Awasthi (2004) observed that firms in clusters have shown higher productivity both in national as also international context as compared to their counterpart industries situated in isolated areas and not in clusters. It has also been observed that being clustered, MSMEs choose networking and collective action as a strategy to access market, credit, infrastructure, R&D, etc which are required by individual units but cannot be obtained through individual efforts. Similarly, it is easier for financial institutions to offer credit at the cluster level in a targeted fashion and with greater assurance of repayment. Literature indicates that these advantages have been obtained in clusters of traditional goods such as textiles, ceramics, furniture, jewelry, leather and leather products, garments etc and also in sophisticated products such as precision machine tools, pharmaceuticals, computer parts, surgical instruments etc. (Foundation for MSME, 2007).

7.3 A Glimpse of Clustering around the Globe

Italy is considered the cradle for cluster development and global understanding of the clustering phenomenon. Clustering, however, is a widespread phenomenon and has been documented in developed and developing countries. The number of clusters in select developed and developing countries (other than India) is given in Table 1.10

Table 1.10: Number of Clusters In Select Developed and Developing Countries (Other than India)

Sl. No.	*Countries*	*No. of Clusters*
	Developed Economies	
1.	Denmark	19
2.	France	95
3.	Germany	31
4.	Italy	199
5.	Japan	18

(Contd...)

6.	Switzerland	13
7.	UK	165
8.	USA	152
9.	Bahrain	3
10.	Bangladesh	23
11.	Brazil	4
12.	China	101
13.	Iran	116
14.	Kuwait	3
15.	Mexico	7
16.	Oman	24
17.	Pakistan	43
18.	Qatar	8
19.	Saudi Arabia	21
20.	Sri Lanka	15
21.	Thailand	35
22.	UAE	17

Note: List of clusters for the individual countries is in no way exhaustive and is a function of the extent of data gathered by this study. Again, since data for India is quite exhaustive, author has shown it separately, lest it should not bias the table.

Source: Foundation for MSME clusters, (2007) based on [a) P, Bianchi, et al. (1996), b) http:// igedrein.org/solar/solar_sre_clustern\vill.htm,c) www.smeda.org.pk,d) www.ahan.org.pke) www.competitiveness.lk/ ceramics.htm, f) Linde Class Van Der (2002), g) OECD. (2007)]

Italy, the country which pioneered cluster development initiatives in the world has the highest number of clusters, followed by UK and USA among select countries. Among the developing countries, Iran has the highest number of clusters, followed by China. However, it is pertinent to note that data on Indian clusters have not been included in this table as the data for India is exhaustive.

Hi-tech clusters signify clusters with high levels of technology such as IT and IT Enabled Services, computers, biotechnology and related services, precision instruments and avionics. Traditional manufacturing clusters comprised of non hi-tech and non micro clusters, and micro enterprises clusters included low-tech poverty intensive clusters such as handlooms, handicrafts and other micro enterprises.

The table further shows that an overwhelming majority of clusters in Asia (69.7 percent), Africa (91.7 percent), Europe (89 Per cent), North America (87.5 percent) and Latin & South America (82.8 percent) were traditional manufacturing clusters. In the Australian sub-continent there was almost equal number of hi-tech and traditional manufacturing clusters.

It is observed that 82.8 percent of the total clusters mapped world over was traditional manufacturing clusters, 11.8 percent were hi tech clusters and only 5.4 percent were artisanal clusters.

7.4. Cluster Development Initiatives in Sericulture

Sericulture- a rural based, high employment generating, profitable enterprise plays a vital role in the socio- economic development of a country like India. Also being an excellent foreign exchange earner, silk industry ought to excel by producing quality bivoltine silk to beat the challenges of the changed global marketing trends especially in the backdrop of the post-*Multi Fiber Arrangement* (MFA) and *WTO* regime. For pursuing such an ambitious goal of bivoltine sericulture development, a well knit/planned extension system was the need of the hour, in order to effectively transfer the new bivoltine technologies to the stakeholders so as to reach the targeted production of quality bivoltine silk. To achieve this task, a full proof extension mechanism that is holistic, decentralized, loaded with information, and participatory in nature, with demand driven system was on exploration by Central Silk Board. Adding to it over the years CSRTI, Mysore was quietly test verifying various extension approaches to widen its transfer of technology (ToT) ambit among sericulturists. Towards this "Cluster approach" based on strong "Researcher – Extension worker – Farmer" (R-E-F) linkage proved the best. Instilling this very "Cluster approach" confidence among all the players in sericulture development in the country, an ambitions "Cluster Promotion Programme" (CPP) was launched by Central Silk Board and implemented during XI jointly with state sericultural departments organizing 50 sericulture clusters covering both mulberry and *Vanya* sectors spread over 17 states for the promotion of sericulture especially the bivoltine. Of these 31 clusters pertained to mulberry sector in the entire country including 22 of them to be implemented in Southern India. It is most heartening to place on record that the Cluster Promotion Programme is concluded most successfully with an ever highest quantum of 1 crore 11 lakh Bivoltine Dfls reared harvesting on an average 65 kg of cocoons/100 dfls against the overall benchmark of 49.18 kg/100 dfls recording an amazing improvement of 32%. In the peninsular India, Karnataka, AP, TN and Maharashtra, the programme was launched in the year 2008-09 in 14 clusters followed by eight more in 2009-10. It's contribution towards promotion and sustenance of bivoltine silk especially in South India with first time crossing 1000 MT BV silk production mark during the project period has been remarkable! CSRTI Mysore was responsible for the successful handling of 22 clusters out of 50 in close coordination of respective DOS in the region. The program in fact, has also supported the continuance of the benefits derived in the JICA assisted projects as well as Institute Village Linkage Programs in promotion of bivoltine sericulture (CSB, 2012).

Cluster promotion approach has emerged during the last decade as one of the most innovative and effective ways for the development of land based enterprises among the developed as well as the developing countries. In the cluster promotion approach, a cluster of villages and families located nearby are selected and adopted so as to have area/mass effect of the improved technologies introduced under the programme and the programmes are manageable by the limited scientists and extension workers jointly with the active involvement of local stakeholders. Under this programme, contiguous villages (if more than one village) within the radius of around 20 km in order were selected to save time and money on transport and to facilitate closer interactions of scientists and extension personnel of CSB and DOS with the adopted families. This helped in effective supervision and guidance by the scientists extension personnel of CSB and DOS. One village or a cluster of villages located nearby was selected in such a way that as far as possible all eligible families of village/cluster of villages were covered under the programme. About 100 to 200 families (beneficiaries) were selected from such village /villages. Adopted village/villages were regarded as a field operational unit and all eligible farm families including big, medium and small farmers irrespective of caste and creed were the beneficiaries of the programme. The inputs to support plantation, rearing houses construction and silkworm rearings were provided under CDP scheme of CSB through respective DOS in each state where as training and guidance were provided by main Institute to all farmers of the field operational units (CSB, 2012).

During XII Plan, the foremost thrust was to augment the import substitute silk in the country and to increase the production of BV silk to 5000 MT from the production level of 1685 MT (2011-12). To achieve the target, Central Silk Board in association with State Sericulture Departments had organized 172 Bivoltine Clusters and achieved production of 5266 MT Bivoltine silk at the end of XII Plan, which includes 3405 MT production through clusters. Cluster Promotion Programme is being continued from 2017-18 to 2019-20 mainly to focus on enhancing the Country's bivoltine raw silk production target of 8500 MT at the end of 2019-20. While restructuring/reorientation of some of the existing clusters of Northwestern region for effective monitoring purpose the total number of clusters were brought down to 151clusters from the existing 172 clusters without effecting the total cluster target.

With the joint concentrated efforts, 5874 MTs of Bivoltine raw silk has been produced against Country's target of 6200 MTs during 2017-18 (11.5 % increase over 5266 MT produced in 2016-17). Bivoltine clusters contributed 4100 MT (70.0%) out of the country's total BV raw silk production of 5874MT. During 2018-19 the total BV raw silk production stands at 6911 MT out of which 151 clusters contributed 4987 MT (72.16%). (CSB, 2019).

7.4.1 Cluster Development in Sericulture in Mizoram

In pursuance of the suggestion from the Planning Commission and Ministry of Textiles, Government of India, Central Silk Board (CSB) and Departments of Sericulture (DOS) of selected states has initiated Cluster Promotion Programme during 2007-12. The CBS and DOS have jointly identified 45 model sericulture clusters in pre-cocoon sector during 2008-09 and 2009-10, in 16 States including Mizoram. The sericulture department of Mizoram has selected 10 clusters under the 'Cluster area development project' namely Khamrang, Saitual, Darlung, Kanghmun, Khawhai, Serchhip, Zobawk, Rotlang, Bawktlang and Lungbun as on 2011-12 (Directorate of Sericulture, Government of Mizoram, 2012).

References

Awasthi, D. (2004). *Labour Process and Productivity in Micro and Small Enterprises (MSEs): the Indian Experience.* Paper presented at the 46th Annual Labour Economics Conference, organised by Institute of Development Studies, Jaipur.

Bhat, T.A., & Choure, T. (2014). An economic analysis of mulberry raw silk production in traditional and non-traditional states of India. *World Journal of Economic and Finance,* 1(3), 016-020.

Bhushi, U.M., & Pharsiyawar, S.M. (2004). Some perspectives in Silk and Powerloom Textile Industry- A Case Study. *International Engineering Management Conference.* Harvard University, Working paper, pp. 1-62.

Cantillon, R. (1755). *Essai sur la nature du commerce en general* (ed. H. Higgs) London: Macmillan (1931).

Central Silk Board. (2012). *Functioning of Central Silk Board and Performance of Indian Silk Industry.* Central Silk Board, Ministry of Textiles, Govt. of India. Retrieved from http://texmin.nic.in/sites/default/files/note-on-sericulture-EnglishOct2018.pdf.

Central Silk Board. (2018). Retrieved from http://csb.gov.in/assets/Uploads/pdf-files/CSBAR-1415English.pdf.

Central Silk Board. (2019). *Functioning of Central Silk Board and Performance of Indian Silk Industry*. Central Silk Board, Ministry of Textiles, Govt. of India. Retrieved from http://texmin.nic.in/sites/default/files/note-on-sericulture-EnglishOct2018.pdf.

Census of India. (2011). Retrieved from: http://www.censusindia.gov.in/2011Census/pes/Pesreport.pdf

Choudhury, B.N., Engzananga, D., Vanlallawma, C., Pachuau, L., Deori, S., & Biswas, T.K. (2013). Development of Sericulture in Mizoram: An alternative source of livelihood for the Tribal Communities. Souvenir and compendium, 1st Bodoland National Seminar-cum-workshop on Sericulture industry and its role in the socioEconomic Upliftment in Rural Society, 10-11 August 2013, pp. 139-145.

Choudhury, B.N., Das, S.C., & Ahmed M. (2017). Studies on Knowledge and Adoption Level of Sericultural Technologies among the Farmers of Aizawl District of Mizoram. *Imperial Journal of Interdisciplinary Research,* 3(5), 1573-1578.

Cuervo, A., Ribeiro, D., & Roig, S. (2005). *Entrepreneurship: concepts, theory and perspective.*Retrieved from http://www.uv.es/bcjauveg/docs/ LibroCuervo RibeiroRoigIntroduction.pdf.

Das, R., & Das, K. (2011). Industrial cluster: An approach for rural development in North East India. International *Journal of Trade, Economics and Finance,* 2(2), 15-32.

Directorate of Economics and Statistics. (2012). *Statistical handbook*, Mizoram, Directorate of Economics and Statistics, Government of Mizoram.

Directorate of Sericulture: Aizawl, Mizoram. (2012). *Sericulture at a glance*, Information and Publicity Cell, Government of Mizoram.

Drucker, P.F. (1985). *Innovation and Entrepreneurship*, Oxford: Butterworth Heinemann, 1985.

Foundation for MSME Clusters. (2007). Policy and Status Paper on Cluster Development in India. Retrieved from www.msmefoudation.org.

Foundation for MSME Clusters. (2009). Clustering for Progress: The Road Traveled and The Way Ahead. Retrieved from www.msmefoundation.org.

Government of India. (2013). *Annual Report 2012-13*, Central Silk Board, Ministry of Textiles, Government of India, Bangalore.

Government of Karnataka. (2011). *Integrated agribusiness development policy*, Department of agriculture, Government of Karnataka, Bangalore.

Government of Mizoram. (2011). *Mizoram Remote Sensing Application Centre (MIRSAC)*, Science & Technology, Planning Department, Government of Mizoram.

Government of Mizoram. (2014. *Economic Survey, 2013-14,* Planning & Programme Implementation Department.

Mittal R. (2006). Entrepreneurship development through agripreneurship in India: Crossing the boundaries with Agri-Export Zones (AEZ) National Institute of Agricultural Marketing, Agribusiness & Entrepreneurship Cell.

Narasaiah, M.L. (2003). Problems and prospects of sericulture. Discovery Publishing House, New Delhi.

NCEUS. (2009). Retrieved from: www.nceus.gov.in

OECD. (2007). *Reviews of Regional Innovation, Competitive Regional Clusters, National policy Approaches*, OECD.

Panday, P.N., Sharan S.K., & Mishra, P.K. (2005). *A biochemical approach: Silk culture*. APH Publishing Corporation, New Delhi.

Porter, M. (1998). Clusters and the New Economics of Competition. *Harvard Business Review*, 76(6), November-December, 77–91.

Ramswamy, R., & Kumar J. N.V.R. (2011). Impact of cluster on entrepreneurship in tribal artisan clusters: A case study of Thenzawl handloom cluster, Mizoram. *SEDME,* 38(2), 39-51.

Rani, G.S. (2006). *Women in sericulture*. Discovery Publishing House, New Delhi.

Rathnam, N., Narasaiah, P.V., & Murthy, S.D. (2013). Current status of silk industry in India – An evaluation. *SEDME*, 40(4), 55-67.

Rathnam, N.V., & Narasaiah, P.V. (2012). Sericulture Industry – A Boon for Rural Poor: Special Focus on Chittoor District of A.P. *SEDME* 39(3), 17-33.

Rosenfeld, S. (1997). Bringing Business Clusters into the Mainstream of Economic Development. *European Planning Studies*, 5, 3–23.

Sastry, D. U. (1984), op.cit., pp. 89-92.

Say, J.B. (1803). *A Treatise on Political Economy: or, the Production, Distribution and Consumption of Wealth*, New York: Augustus M. Kelley (1964).

Schmitz, H. (1995). Small Shoemakers and Fordist Giants: Tale of a Super cluster. *World Development*, 23(1), 9–28.

Schumpeter, J. (1934). *The theory of economic development*, Harvard University Press.

Singh, T. (2012). Sericulture, Applied Zoology. Retrieved from http://www.gonder.org.tr/wp-content/uploads/2016/04/sericulture-silkwormgenel-bilgi.pdf.

Thiripura K and Ramalakshmi P, (2018), "Silk Production: The Global Scenerio", Asian Review of Social Sciences, Vol. 7, No. 2, pp. 22-24.

Umesh, K.B., Akshara, M., Shripad, B., Harish, Kumar., & Srinivasan, S.M.(2009). Performance Analysis of Production and Trade of Indian Silk under WTO Regime. Contributed Paper prepared for presentation at the International Association of Agricultural Economists Conference, Beijing, China, August 16-22, 2009.

UNIDO. (2001). Women Entrepreneurship Development in Selected African Countries, Working Paper No.7.

Chapter - 2

The Present Study

This chapter has focused on the research problem. Need for the study, the statement of the problem, a review of literature covering the areas of entrepreneurship, clusters and sericulture, the research design which includes the objectives of the study, the methodology adopted are discussed in the following section.

1. Need for the Study

Sericulture industry is an excellent avenue for employment with various entrepreneurial opportunities. India lives in villages and Sericulture being an agro-based enterprise, plays a predominant role in shaping the economic destiny of the rural people and fits very well in the India's rural structure, where agriculture continues to be the main occupation. The pursuit of sericulture offers gainful employment not only for the rural masses but also for the educated youth in semi-urban and urban areas. Growth of sericulture will certainly lead to vibrant rural economy by creating income generating entrepreneurial opportunities enabling poverty reduction.

Mizoram is one of the most promising states for development of Sericulture in North East India where all the four varieties of silk producing food plants are grown and silkworms are reared for silk production. The total production of mulberry cocoons during 2012-13 was 314.37 metric tonnes (Government of Mizoram, 2014).

According to a report of Mizoram Remote Sensing Application Centre (MIRSAC), a project jointly conducted by the North East Space Application Centre (NESAC) and MIRSAC, under the sponsorship of Central Silk Board (CBS) 1439 square kilometers of the State is suitable for mulberry cultivation and 8322 square kilometers are suitable for rearing non-mulberry silk worms. The report was prepared on the basis of data through remote sensing and geographical information system (Government of Mizoram, 2011).

Over the years sericulture is playing a vital role in development of the rural economy of Mizoram, in terms of employment opportunities. Mizoram occupies the 17th place in respect of area under mulberry, cocoon and silk raw production in India during 2011-2012 (Rathnam, Narasaiah and Murthy, 2013). The total area under mulberry and the total cocoon production was 2170 and 1650 hectares respectively and raw silk production during the period was 24 metric tonnes. Presently 12,000 farmers are practicing sericulture as an occupation in Mizoram (Directorate of Sericulture, 2012). A few years ago sericulture was considered a subsidiary occupation of farmers with small ownership. Now it is no longer a subsidiary occupation and more farmers are taking it up as an occupation.

However, it was observed that in spite of all the advantage that the State of Mizoram has for the development of Sericulture, the growth of Sericulture industry has been at a very slow pace and the reasons could be attributed to lack of infrastructural facilities, paucity of fund, inadequate personnel and non-traditional practice of Sericulture activities. (Government of Mizoram, 2014)

2. Review of Literature

The main objective of this section is to review the available literature on entrepreneurship, clusters and sericulture industry. Relevant literature in respect of these three important areas was drawn to understand the current status of research on entrepreneurship in sericulture sector in Mizoram.

2.1. Studies on Entrepreneurship

In this section the researcher has attempted to trace the history of entrepreneurship and reviewed significant studies on different facets of entrepreneurship relevant to the present study.

2.1.1. A Historical Perspective

The word entrepreneur is derived from the root French word '*entreprendre*', which means, 'to undertake'. The meaning of the word dates back to Cantillon (1755) and has been defined in myriad hues over the centuries. Some important contributors to the evolution of the term were Say (1803), who referred to an entrepreneur as an organiser, Knight (1942) who described him or her as risk bearer and Cole (1959) who defined entrepreneurship as "the purposeful activity of an individual or group of associated individuals, undertaken to initiate, maintain or aggrandize profit by production or distribution of economic goods and services." Schumpeter

(1934) described the entrepreneur as an innovator who carried out new combinations. Theses new combinations could take the form of introduction of a new product, a new method of production, exploring a new market, conquest of a new source of supply of materials and carrying out of a new organisation of industry. McClelland (1961) emphasised on the need for achievement. According to him an entrepreneur with high n-achievement takes personal responsibility for finding solutions to problems, sets moderate achievement goals and takes calculated risks; and wants concrete feedback on his performance.

The term entrepreneur evolved different meanings in later years. Drucker (1985) defined an entrepreneur as one who always searches for change, responds to it and exploits it as an opportunity. He opined that innovation is a tool of entrepreneurship, which endows resources with a new capacity to create wealth and discussed seven sources of opportunities namely, the unexpected, the incongruity,innovation based on process need, changes in industry structure or market structure, demographics (population changes), changes in perception, mood and, new knowledge.

2.1.2. Entrepreneurship in India

Many researchers have studied different dimensions of entrepreneurship in India. Berna (1960) studied fifty manufacturing enterprises in Tamil Nadu and observed that caste and tradition do not play an important role in the emergence of entrepreneurship.

Gaikwad and Tripathi (1970) studied entrepreneurs in Andhra Pradesh and found that all the entrepreneurs had drive, initiative and were hardworking. Sharma (1975) conducted a survey on 245 entrepreneurs from Punjab and Uttar Pradesh and concluded that government policies play a crucial role to sustain the interest of entrepreneurs in the continuous expansion of business. Hundal (1977) studied the entrepreneurial motivation of 434 entrepreneurs from various towns of Punjab and observed that the entrepreneurs were motivated by concern about self, social repute, remote rewards and conscience.

Nafziger (1978) studied fifty four manufacturing enterprises in Vishakhapatnam and concluded that a high number of successful entrepreneurs belonged to families of the brahmans and families with a high economic status.

Gangadhara Rao (1986) ascertained and evaluated the impact of industrial estates on the emergence of entrepreneurship in Coastal Andhra.

He concluded that though the impact of industrial estates on the emergence of entrepreneurship in Coastal Andhra was marginal, a new sense of awareness about the virtues of self employment through industrial entrepreneurship is emerging among agricultural communities, white collared workmen and unemployed. However, he observed that artisans and factory workers needed to be awakened and brought into the fold of entrepreneurship.

Khanka (1990) defined entrepreneurship as "an attempt to create value through recognition of business opportunity, the management of risk-taking appropriate to the opportunity, and through communicative and management skills to mobilise human, financial and material resources necessary to bring a project to fruition."

Manimala (1999) explored the phenomenon of entrepreneurial heuristics (rules of thumb) and provided insights into what "pioneering innovators" do while establishing and operating their enterprises. Manimala's study moved away from the focus on 'what the entrepreneur is' to 'what the entrepreneur does.'

2.1.3 Entrepreneurship in North East India

Here the researcher has reviewed the few but significant studies conducted on entrepreneurship in NER.

Baruah (2000) conducted a study on 140 successful women entrepreneurs who were trained in six states of NER viz, Assam, Megahalaya, Manipur, Tripura, Arunachal Pradesh and Mizoram to find out the impact of the efforts of the training institutions to create entrepreneurs in the North East. She concluded that successful women entrepreneurs in the North East transcend communities and castes and that most of these entrepreneurs were supported by their families to adopt entrepreneurship as a career.

Das (2000) conducted a study on women entrepreneurs in Kamrup district (Greater Guwahati city) in Assam and concluded that most of the entrepreneurs had entered business through choice, were educated and had high n-achievement.

Mali (2000) conducted a study on trained women entrepreneurs belonging to some states in NER and concluded that support from their family members; in case of married entrepreneurs, husbands and in case of unmarried women, parents played an important role in their becoming successful entrepreneurs. He observed that there was an emerging trend of women entrepreneurship in NER and there was an urgent need to support this trend.

Srivastav and Syngkon (2007) conducted a study in a tribal district in East Khasi hills of Meghalaya to analyse the various emerging aspects of SSIs and observed that most of the SSIs are adopting direct selling marketing strategy rather than indirect selling strategy and produce the products mainly to cater to the local market demand. A majority of entrepreneurs were educated and first generation tribal entrepreneurs and more than one fourth of them were women entrepreneurs. However, these small industries were at the preliminary stage of development and had yet to make a significant contribution to the growth of the economy in Meghalaya in a significant way.

Entrepreneurial motivation in Assam was studied by Khanka (2009) on a sample of 243 first generation entrepreneurs and he observed that the entrepreneurs were primarily motivated by the need for economic achievement, personal growth, autonomy and recognition. No significant difference was found on gender basis. He also observed significant changes in autonomy and power motives as the entrepreneurs gained experience over a period of time transforming their role from doers to implementers, as their enterprises grew.

Few studies are available on industrialisation and economic development of Mizoram. Some of the notable works were conducted by Lianzela (1994, 1995) that focused on the economic development of Mizoram and Agarwal (1999) on industries in Mizoram. Kabra (2008) studied the role of business and industry in the economic growth of Mizoram. Laskar (2010) studied the problems and prospects of industrial development with a focus on small and cottage industries in the State. Lalhriatpuii (2010) in her study focused on economic participation of women including some entrepreneurs in Mizoram. However, there seems to be no substantive evidence of research work exclusively on woman entrepreneurship among artisans in the State of Mizoram.

2.2. Studies on Clusters

Researchers, academics and policy makers have evinced great interest in clustering. Many facets of clustering viz, advantages of clustering, cluster development, cluster initiatives, and so on have been researched upon. The researcher in this section has attempted to review some important studies relevant to the present study.

2.2.1. Conceptual framework

The clustering of firms is rooted in Marshall's (1907, 1919) analysis of industrial districts. He observed that several advantages such as a pool of specialisedlabour, access to suppliers of specialised inputs and services, and dissemination of inventions, new ideas and improvements in technology can be derived by enterprises following the same type of business in the same geographical locality.

This conceptualisation of clusters was followed by a lot of research interest, stimulated by the success of the 'industrial districts' of Italy which popularly came to be known as 'third Italy'. Becattini (1991), Piore and Sabel (1984) traced the success of the industrial clusters of 'Third Italy' and provided an impetus to research on clusters in 1990s. Becattini (1991) interpreted Marshallian industrial districts as 'socio-territorial entities' which were characterised by the active presence of both a community of people and enterprises in a common area, naturally and historically bounded.

Porter (1990) modeled the effect of the local business environment on competition in terms of inter related influences, graphically depicted in a diamond popularly known as the 'diamond theory.' The theory explained that a cluster is the manifestation of the diamond at work, comprising of three elements viz, proximity arising from the co-location of companies, customers, and suppliers and other institutions.

Porter (1998) in his book 'On Competition' defined clusters as geographic concentrations of inter connected companies and institutions in a particular field and explained why clusters are critical to competition, mapped selected clusters in the U.S.A and Portugal and elaborated on the roles to be played by governments both national and local in cluster development.

2.2.2. Studies on clustering around the globe

Academic literature in the following years thereafter has focused on different perspectives of clustering in developed and developing countries. Some of the significant research works on developed countries include the studies by Piore and Sabel, (1984); Best (1990); Brusco (1982) and Becattini (1991); Mitsui (2003) and Higgins (1998).

Academic research work also extended to clusters in developing countries such as footwear cluster of Agra, Uttar Pradesh in India (Knorringa, 1998), cluster of shoemakers of Sinos valley in Brazil (Schmitz, 1995), shoe cluster of Leoan and Guadalajara in Mexico (Rabelloti, 1993, 1995), textile cluster of Diego in Korea (Cho, 1994), cotton knitwear cluster of Tirupur, Tamil Nadu in India (Cawthorne, 1995). Some other notable research studies were: engineering and electronics cluster of Bangalore, Karnataka in India (Holmstrom, 1993), diamond cluster of Surat, Gujarat in India (Kashyap, 1992), surgical instruments cluster of Sialkot in Pakistan (Nadvi 1995). Das (1999) made a comparative analysis of a developed cluster namely pump manufacturing cluster of Coimbatore (Tamil Nadu) and a 'developing cluster' namely, rubber manufacturing cluster of Kottayam (Kerala) and hand tool clusters in Jalandhar and Ludhiana (Punjab) and Nagaur (Rajasthan). Das (2003) further conducted a study on the garment cluster of Ahmedabad in India. Pal and Sood (2004) conducted a study on the flooring cluster of Morbi town (Gujarat). UNIDO's cluster development programmes, probably the most widely publicized initiatives has conducted diagnostic studies and prepared Cluster Action Plan for many clusters in the developing countries (www.unido.org).

2.3. Studies on Agripreneurs

Literature has often excluded farmers from the realm of entrepreneurship. As rightly observed by Puera et al (2002) part of this recognition gap comes from agricultural tradition itself, as farmers do not think themselves as entrepreneurs. Carter (1998) and Mc Nally (2001) argued that some methods used to study entrepreneurs could be used to study farmers. Townsend, (2013) observed that farmers over the world are economic agents, dealing with cost, returns and risks. Within their small individual allocative domain they are fine tuning entrepreneurs, tuning so subtly that many experts fail to recognize how efficient they are. Although farmers differ for reasons of schooling, health and experience in their ability to perceive, to interpret and to take appropriate action in responding to new information, they provide an essential human resource, which is entrepreneurship.

Dollinger (1995) defines entrepreneurship in agriculture as the creation of an innovative economic organization for the purpose of growth or gain under conditions of risk and uncertainty in agriculture. Gray (2002) viewed entrepreneurship in agriculture is important for more productivity and profitability of agriculture.

Indian agriculture is low in productivity with large number of disguised unemployment. Providing viable and sustainable business opportunities in Indian agribusiness is essential for generating employment in the country.

Agripreneurship may also be defined as generally sustainable, community oriented, directly marketed agriculture. Sustainable agriculture denotes a holistic, systemoriented approach to forming that focuses on the interrelationship of social, economic and environmental process. So an agripreneur can simply means an entrepreneur whose main business is agriculture or agriculture related (Nagalakshmi, 2013) Agripreneurship is greatly influenced by three factors namely, the economic situation, education and culture in India (Tripathi& Agarwal, 2015).

An agripreneur may also be defined as someone who undertakes a variety of agricultural activities and its allied sectors. An agripreneur may start an agro-business, change a business direction, acquire a business or may be involved in innovatory activity of value addition. He is a risk taker, opportunist, initiator, which deals with uncertain agricultural business environment of the farm. (Tripathi & Agarwal, 2015).

Elwee (2007) studied agripreneurs in Finland, where the farmers perceived themselves as growth-oriented, risk-taker, innovative, optimistic and having more personal control of their business activities. He defined agripreneurs as those occupied on a part or full time basis on a range of activities which are primarily dependent on the farm and by agriculture, by which means practice of cultivating the soil, growing crops and raising livestock as the main source of income.

Singh (2012) contended that agripreneurs are not just farmers, but also thinkers, risk takers and business people. To make this approach successful, the researcher suggested all aspects such as cultural, social and political situations must be addressed in a holistic way.

Bairwa et al (2014) opined that agripreneurship have the potential to contribute to a range of social and economic development such as employment generation, income generation, poverty reduction and improvement in nutrition, health and overall food security in the national economy. It also has the potential to generate growth, diversify income, providing widespread employment and entrepreneurial opportunities in rural areas. Agripreneurship is the need of the hour to make agriculture more attractive and profitable venture.

Narendran (2015) reported that agripreneurship is basically doing entrepreneurial activities in agriculture and related areas. He suggested youth of the rural areas should pursue agripreneurship for better employment and social status.

Wayne and Philip, 2007 conducted a meta_ analysis of studies that contrast the achievement motivation of entrepreneurs and managers. The results indicate that entrepreneurs exhibit higher achievement motivation than managers and that these differences are influenced by the entrepreneur's venture goals, by the use of U.S. or foreign samples, and, to a less clear extent, by projective or objective instrumentation. Moreover, when the analysis is restricted to venture founders, the difference between entrepreneurs and managers on achievement motivation is substantially larger and the credibility intervals do not include zero.

2.4. Studies on Entrepreneurial Motivations

Khanka (2009) did study on entrepreneurial motivation based on a sample of 243 first-generation entrepreneurs in Assam in North-East India. The results clearly showed that the entrepreneurs were primarily motivated by the need for economic achievement, personal growth, autonomy and recognition.

One way to explain entrepreneurial aspiration levels is by means of motives (Kolvereid 1992; Amit et al 2001; Morris et al 2006; Cassar 2007). The entrepreneurial process occurs because people are motivated to pursue and exploit perceived opportunities. It is rooted in the theory that action is the result of motivation and cognition (Diana et al, 2012). Locke and Latham (1990) observed that motivation refers to factors within an individual, other than knowledge, which energize, direct and sustain behavior. According to Bird (1988), entrepreneurial motivation is manifested in the entrepreneur's vision and goals and it bears upon planning and behavior.

Several drivers of entrepreneurial aspirations and entrepreneurial motivations are investigated by Hessesl et al (2008) using country-level data from the Global Entrepreneurship Monitor (GEM) for the years 2005 and 2006. They estimated a two-equation model explaining aspirations using motivations and socioeconomic variables, and explaining motivations using socioeconomic variables. It was found that countries with a higher incidence of increase-wealth-motivated entrepreneurs tend to have a higher prevalence of high-job-growth and export-oriented entrepreneurship and that a country's level of social security relates negatively to the prevalence of innovative, high-job-growth, and export-oriented entrepreneurship. It was also found that the increase-wealth motive mediates the relationship between socioeconomic variables and entrepreneurial aspirations.

Ostwald et al (2012) describes the existing options, areal extents, and Swedish farmers' conditions for energy crop production promoted by the governments to mitigate and adapt to climate change. The drivers of and barriers to cultivating various energy crops are described in terms of a variety of motivational factors. It was found that economic motivations for changing production systems are strong, but factors such as values (e.g., esthetic), knowledge (e.g., habits and knowledge of production methods), and legal conditions (e.g., cultivation licenses) are crucial for the change to energy crops.

Ramswamy and Kumar (2012) observed that the weavers of Thenzawl cluster, located in Serchhip district of Mizoram, have redefined the quintessential'marginalized weaver' as a strongly motivated woman entrepreneur who has transformed the role of weaving from a mere wage-earning activity or a domestic chore to a commercially viable enterprise, regardless of the number of looms owned.

2.5. Studies on Sericulture

Acharya's (1993) study focussed on certain specific problems in sericultural expansion relating mainly to local climatic factors, excess irrigation leading to water logging, and problems relating to extension support and marketing of cocoons, covering two clusters one in the district of Mysore and the other in the district of Shimoga. He observed that lack of skill in sericulture, absence of space to rear silkworms and lack of extension support were the main problems faced by the farmers.

Indian Institute of Entrepreneurship (2005) in its Evaluation cum Impact Study of STEP Project for Handloom Weavers of Assam analysed the project on some basic parameters and found major gaps in the sustained operation of the project in North East India. The study included beneficiaries from sericulture villages spread over Assam namely Kamrup, Nagaon, Jorhat, Sibsagar, Golaghat, Dibrugarh, Morigaon, Baska, Nalbari and Barpata. The report recommended clustered approach towards beneficiaries and a strict adherence to the criteria of selecting poor asset-less rural women as beneficiaries. The report also recommended the criteria for selection of beneficiaries, their training; implementation of the project; and modus operandi for distribution of materials and financial support.

Rani (2006) conducted her study in Rayalaseema region of Andhra Pradesh where she highlighted the role of women in various activities involved in raising mulberry crop and rearing of silk worm. The study supported the argument that sericulture is a highly profitable income generating activity to elevate the status of rural poor especially women.

Rathnam and Narsaiah (2012) made a conceivable attempt to analytically examine the growth and development of sericulture industry in Chittoor district in Andhra Pradesh. They found that sericulture has come to be regarded as one of the means of alleviating rural poverty and ushering in rural prosperity in the district in terms of employment and income generation. However, the industry was confronted with a plethora of problems in production, finance and marketing and there was an urgent need to allocate funds and implement the development schemes and programmes more effectively to enliven the sericulture industry in the district.

Raymond and Habiyaremye (2013) assessed the impact of developing sericulture on enhancing farmers income and reducing poverty among farmers in Rwanda in Africa. Sericulture though a relatively recent phenomenon in Rwandan farming activities has emerged as an agricultural technological innovation. Their study indicated that the poverty reduction effects of sericulture adoption was still very low, but acknowledged the limitations of such an estimation at an early adoption stage.

Rathnam, Narasaiah and Murthy (2013) examined the origin, growth and development, problems and prospects of silk industry in India. They found that India has tremendous unexploited potential for silk development and at the same time industry has been confronting different problems and impediments. They offered suggestions that would prove a gate-way to the propensity of the industry

According to Kasi (2013) Sericulture has brought about overall development of individual households, the village, and the community at large in KothaIndlu village, Chittoor District of Andhra Pradesh in South India where sericulture is an important means for generating employment, income enhancement crop enterprises, He observed that women were playing an important role in silk rearing and processing activities and performed their skillfully.

According to Rama Rao (1978), one hectare of sericulture which included mulberry cultivation and silkworm rearing would provide employment for at least two families of five persons each.

Sathish (1985), based on their study in Pithepuram block of East Godavari, Andra Pradesh concluded that dairy sericulture farming system with adequate credit facilities created the highest employment opportunity than diary farming system. While assessing the employment potential in sericulture in India, Krishna swamy (1986), found that about five persons could be engaged in one acre of mulberry garden throughout the year under Indian conditions.

Kumara swamy B.K. (1993), observed that sericulture is being labour intensive, it is eminently suited to the economy of the small farms ensuring high employment opportunities to 664 man days of family labour to total labour per acre as compare to only 381 for alternative crops. Jaganathan L. (1996), Indicated that sericulture provided more employment opportunites to family labour that is 70 % of total labour compared to alternative crops 44 % only.

Employment generation is one of the major potentials of Sericulture and Silk Industry in India. The farm and non-farm activity of this sector creates sixty lakh mandays of employment every year mostly in rural sector. In West Bengal, more than one lakh families are occupied with sericulture activities where Karnataka is the state with the largest number of families involved with sericulture. Despite having high level family involvement, West Bengal produces smaller quantities of raw silk compared to Karnataka as well as Andhra Pradesh. Roy et al (2012) investigated the reason of this low production and finds out that low productivity of land is no way responsible for that. Different Employment Models constructed in their study suggest that 'area of mulberry cultivation', 'cocoon-market' and 'power-looms' are powerful factors in changing the level of employment, while the primary survey exposes factors like 'unitary household structure', 'income' 'years of education' and 'numbers of female in the household' as the significant factors in accelerating average employment per family.

According to Murthy (1978), the total cost of establishment was Rs. 1675 per hectare of mulberry, while the total cost of cocoon production was Rs. 14082 per hectare of which 93 percent was the operational cost. The net return from mulberry cultivation was Rs. 7430, while it was Rs. 8202 from cocoon production. The gross and net returns per Kg. of cocoons was Rs. 18.83 and Rs. 7.27 respectively.

Garg (1979), found that mulberry would provide a net return of Rs. 15,715 per hectare, per annum under Indian conditions, while the net income per hectare from other crops was Rs. 3,137 from jute, Rs. 4,056 from paddy and wheat Rs. 1,424. Further, he observed that one hectare of mulberry employment to about 12 man years.

Rajagopalan (1980) in his study in Tamil Nadu, observed that sericulture capable of providing Rs. 15,700 gross income per hectare per year as against Rs. 3,800 from jute and Rs. 7,000 from cotton.

Rajapurohith and Govidaraju (1981), investigated the employment and income potential in sericulture in Mysore and Kolar districts of Karnataka. The results shows that out of Rs. 9,166 house hold income, Rs. 7638 was from sericulture and thus the sericulture income accounted for 83.33 percent of the total house hold income under rainfed conditions. On the other hand, in the irrigated condition 77.3 percent of the total family income of Rs. 19,043 was from sericulture. The employement of human labour per acre of mulberry cultivation and cocoon production was 191.02 man days on irrigated sericulture farms, while it was 166.68 man days per acre on rainfed farms.

Chandrashekar Reddy (1990), reported that the total cost of cocoons production in Hosur taluk, of Tamil Nadu was Rs. 11,972 per acre, per annum of which Rs. 11,206 was the operation cost and the remaining Rs. 766 was the fixed cost. He indicated that the cost of production decreased significantly with the increase in the farm size. The average gross returns from cocoon productionwasRs. 19,997 per acre, per annum and the net return was Rs. 8,025. The net return from sericulture was reported to be 2.6 times higher than that of alternative crops. (Rs. 3.082).

Kumaraswamy B.R.(1992) repoted that, per acre net profit from sericulture was Rs. 32,672 as against Rs.8696 in alternative crops like paddy, Wheat and the percentage of labour cost was found to be 78:46 and 21:52 respectively.

Vishakanta (2018) did a study on cost and return structure of silk rearing farmers in Karnataka. The total cost of production for 100 DFLS was Rs. 22997, with gross returns of Rs. 35128 and net returns of Rs. 12130. Across regions, highest cost was seen in Ramanagara (Rs. 36103), followed by Kanakapura (Rs. 24591) and Channapatna (Rs.20966) whereas net returns was highest in Ramanagara (Rs. 22997), Kanakapura (Rs. 12322) and Channapatna (Rs. 11526). Cost and returns of Bivoltine cocoon production.

The highest cost was incurred by General category of farmers (Rs. 26194) followed by OBC (Rs. 25374), ST (Rs. 23564) and SC (Rs. 23146). The highest net returns was seen among, General (Rs. 14192), followed by OBC (Rs. 13747), SC (Rs.11548) and ST (Rs. 9618). The overall cost and returns was Rs. 24241 and Rs. 12786 respectively. The major reason for practicing the mulberry cultivation is Income throughout the year, followed by employment thought the year, realize more by products and can supplement feed for livestock.

A report of Cluster Promotion Programme (2012) shows that Smt. R Nachammal of Palani Cluster under Cluster Promotion Programme was able to increase mulberry leaf yield from 45,000 kg to 55,000 kg/ha/year enabling herself to take up 10 bivoltine crops with 1480 dfls/acre/year The average yield of 75.44 kg/100 dfls fetches her an annual income of

Rs. 1,33,920. Shri A. Kuppusamy, aged 49 years, is a progressive farmer in Udumalpet Cluster of Tamil Nadu. He owns 2.5 acres land for mulberry cultivation. After being brought under CPP, He rears on an average of 1100 Dfls/acre/year and obtains an average yield of 79.60 kg/100 Dfls. He earned net revenue of 3, 86,673.00 from 2.5 acres of mulberry garden. Though he has a lot of land and cultivating many other crops in his farm, because of his involvement and commitment, he has emerged as a progressive model sericulture farmer in this area. Another report shows that Mr. K.R. Krishna Reddy of V.

Kota cluster of Chittoor District who owns 2.5 acres of mulberry garden 10 crops per year @ 1422 dfls /acre/year and obtains an average cocoon yield of 73.90 kg/100 dfls. He has harvested 1050.60 kg cocoons/acre/year and earned a net revenue of Rs.3, 73,826 from his 2.25 acres farm.

In any discourse on sociology and anthropology, one fact that clearly emerges is that women can generally be trusted to perform their duties with utmost care and attention. This is more so in the case of agriculture and allied activities. No wonder women are playing a very important role in the sericulture industry. Their qualities like maternal instincts and loving care of those under their charge prove to be very helpful in the successful breeding of silk worms. The sericulture industry has opened up phenomenal employment avenues and helped women to become important players in the decisionmaking process—whether in the household or in the community at large. The active involvement of women is very essential for the success of the any community development initiative. This has been proved on many occasions all over the world—more so in the developing countries. Kasi (2013) did an empirical work in KothaIndlu village, Chittoor District of Andhra Pradesh in South India. Sericulture is an important means for generating employment, income enhancement crop enterprises, and is a most appropriate household activity. In all these activities, women have shown their mettle and performed their tasks most skillfully. In the village under study, it was found that women were playing an important role in silk rearing and processing activities. The study showed how “sericulture,” an agro-based activity, has brought about overall development of individual households, the village, and the community at large.

Chowdhury et al. (2011) did a study on women and their contribution share in sericulture ctivities in West Bengal.It was found that availability of facilities at the woman sericulture respondents on their land holding, mulberry areas and rearing houses revealed that 23% of the respondents were having less than 0.5 acre of land, 47% with more than 0.5 acre to

1.0 acre, 23% with more than 1.0 acre to 2.0 acres and 7% were having more than 2.0 acres of land holding. low level of literacy, lack of awareness on the improved technologies of mulberry cultivation and silkworm rearing, poor level of perception on the technologies and lack of powerment are identified as the major constraints faced by the women for sericulture development. The women respondents in various sericulture activities provide ample scopes for their development and capacity building through imparting training, demonstration, awareness of technologies, processes, techniques etc. and guiding them for socio-economically upliftment in the region and the sericulture scenario in the country as well.

Priyadarshani and Kumari (2013) conducted a study in Chittoor district among sericulturists. The study revealed that 6.6 % of the respondents was higher educated, 35.5% respondents were up to secondary level, 32.2% respondents were primary educated and the remaining 25.5% farmers were illiterates.

Dewangan (2017) did a study on sericulture's role to employment generation and socio-economic empowerment of tribal women in Chhattisgarh. He found that more than half of the labour force used in cultivation of mulberry and silkworm rearing was contributed by women labour. Women's participation was high in rearing sector than mulberry cultivation. A great deal of variation exists in their participation across different sericulture regions and socio economic groups and also across their age, status in the household and educational levels.

3. Research Gap

Das (1995) observed that there is a dearth of studies focusing primarily on the 'actual mechanisms' in industrial districts of developing countries. Das (2003) opined that merely a mechanistic and replicative approach to cluster development that ignores the developmental constraints typically faced by the Indian rural economy may fail to succeed in generating employment opportunities as also in creating a competitive and sustainable rural base. He argued that a comprehensive rural development perspective has to be designed within a broader perspective that does not fail to provide an opportunity to the local labour.

In another study, Das (2005) observed that studies on Indian clusters were still very few and for the purpose of both policy and debate on clustering, studies on as many cases as possible would be enriching.

Parilli (2007) observed that research on clusters has not answered the role of survival clusters in developing countries. The researcher classified survival clusters as the kinds of clusters that do not work close to technological frontiers; for example, craft producers who worked independently with little machinery for the local market. Such local systems have often been neglected by researchers, in spite of their density and importance in the economic life of developing countries.

Evidently, there appears to be a dearth of systematic and path finding studies in the area of entrepreneurship in tribal artisan clusters, especially in North east India.

Precisely, the study of entrepreneurship in sericulture cluster is an attempt to fill this gap.

The researcher also observed that a number of studies have been conducted on various aspects of agripreneurship in Mizoram. However, there is no substantive evidence of research done on entrepreneurial aspects in Sericulture clusters in Mizoram. There emerges a need to examine the aspects of agripreneurial motivations, the role of cluster processes and cluster development on agro based industries and their impact on the livelihood of farmers in the religion. The study of entrepreneurship development in sericulture cluster in Mizoram will be an attempt to fill this gap.

4. Research Design

4.1. Statement of the Problem

Entrepreneurship plays a critical role in promoting the economic growth and development in a country. Growth of entrepreneurship in any sector not only improves production systems and thereby productivity but also strengthens the basic foundation of the industry by generating opportunities and employment. Research evidence shows that clustering has an impact on growth of enterprises in clusters. Networking of firms in the cluster is an important advantage derived by the enterprises which, in turn, would create more number of enterprises in the cluster and, as a result, an agglomeration of firms (Ramswamy and Kumar Jyoti, 2011). Sericulture is an agro-based industry and has a very short gestation period, having the potential to generate adequate returns from even small areas of land. It has the potential to provide gainful self-employment to farmer households in rural areas. Keeping in view the impact of clustering for entrepreneurship development and the entrepreneurship potential sericulture offers for the people of Mizoram, this study will focus on various aspects of entrepreneurial development in Saitual sericulture cluster in Mizoram. The proposed study intends to study the motivational factors that have spurred the entrepreneurs to practice sericulture, analyse the business operations of the micro enterprise and examine the role of cluster on the entrepreneurship.

4.2. Objectives of the Study

The objectives of the present study are:-

1. To study the socio-economic profile of agripreneurs of the sericulture cluster.
2. To ascertain the motivational factors of the agripreneurs.
3. To analyse the role of cluster on agripreneurship development.
4. To assess the financial performance of the sericulture enterprises.

4.3. Research Methodolgy

Here it is attempted to specify the scope of the study, the time period for which data was collected from the sample enterprises, sources of data, tools applied for data analysis and limitations of the present study.

Scope of the Study

Saitual Sericulture Cluster

The present study is conducted in Saitual sericulture cluster located 77kms from the capital city, Aizawl. Saitual cluster comprises seven villages viz., Saitual, Keifang, Rulchawm, Maite, North Lungpher, Mualpheng and Sihfa. According to the Census of India (2011), Saitual had a population of 11315, the male population being 5593 and that of female being 5722 and the total number of households is 1522. Saitual enjoys a moderate and pleasant climate. The economy of Saitual is basically agrarian in nature and the major agricultural crops grown are corn, sugarcane and vegetables. Sericulture has become an important occupation in recent years after the cluster started taking its shape in 2009. Saitual has been identified as one among 10 sericulture clusters in Mizoram. Saitual town i.e 97.35 percent (Census, 2011) which is higher than the state average of 91.33 percent. In Saitual, Male literacy is around 97.37 % while female literacy rate is 97.33 % as per Census India 2011. There is one college Saitual College affiliated to Mizoram University (a central university) and several schools.

Sampling

The census method was used where all the 180 farmers were interviewed for the purpose of the present study.

Time period

The researcher collected the primary data through a structured questionnaire, administered to all the agripreneurs (180 in number) engaged in sericulture in Saitual cluster during Dec. 2016 to Feb. 2017.

Sources of Data

The researcher relied on primary data as well as secondary data. The primary data was collected through a structured and discussions with the agripreneurs of the cluster and the Government departments. The structured questionnaire was administered to aadministered to all the agripreneurs (180 in number) engaged in sericulture in Saitual cluster during December 2016 to February 2017.

The questionnaire was translated into Mizo language and the answers to the questionnaires were again translated into English to facilitate analysis. Secondary data was collected from relevant reports, journals, books, newspapers and e-resources. The researcher visited the Central Silk Board (CSB) complex in Bangalore during January 2015 and collected CSB reports and books on sericulture.

An attempt was made to cover all entrepreneurs or enterprises belonging to all the seven villages in the town namely, Saitual, Keifang, Rulchawm, Maite. North Lungpher, Mualpheng and Sihfa as shown in Table 2.1.

The maximum number of entrepreneurs surveyed belonged to Saitual (40 percent), followed by Keifang (35.6 percent) and the least number of entrepreneurs were from Mualpheng (1.1 percent).

Table 2.1: Distribution of agripreneurs in the cluster

Name of the village	*Frequency*	*Percentage*
Saitual	72	40
Keifang	64	35.6
Rulchawm	26	14.4
Maite	5	2.8
North Lungpher	7	3.8
Mualpheng	2	1.1
Sihfa	4	2.3
TOTAL	**180**	**100**

Source: Field Work.

4.4. Hypotheses

Hypotheses were framed to test each motivational factor on the basis of land holding of the agripreneurs classified as small, medium and large. Wherever the hypothesis was rejected the researcher attempted to find out the relationship of that motive vis-à-vis small, medium and large farmers using H Test as a tool.

H_{o1}: There is no significant relationship between the size of the farm holding and the motive 'to earn money'

H_{11}: There is a significnat relationship between the size of the farm holding and the motive 'to earn money'

H_{o1a}: There is no significant relationship between small and medium farmers and the motive 'to earn money'.

H_{11a}: There is a significant relationship between small and medium farmers and the motive 'to earn money'

H_{o1b}: There is no significant relationship between medium and large farmers and the motive 'to earn money'.

H_{11b}: There is a significant relationship between medium and large farmers and the motive 'to earn money'

H_{o2}: There is no significant relationship between the size of the farm holding and the motive 'to earn a a livelihood'

H_{12}: There is a significant relationship between the size of the farm holding and the motive 'to earn a livelihood'.

H_{o3}: There is no significant relationship between the size of the farm holding and the motive 'to give financial security to family'.

H_{13}: There is a significant relationship between the size of the farm holding and the motive 'to give financial security to family'.

H_{o4}: There is no significant relationship between the size of the farm holding and the motive 'enjoyment of work'.

H_{14}: There is a significant relationship between the size of the farm holding and the motive 'enjoyment of work'.

H_{o5}: There is no significant relationship between the size of the farm holding and the motive 'to gain independence'

H_{15}: There is a significant relationship between the size of the farm holding and the motive 'to gain independence'.

H_{06}: There is no significant relationship between the size of the farm holding and the motive 'to diversify my economic interests'.

H_{16}: There is a significant relationship between the size of the farm holding and the motive 'To diversify my economic interests'.

H_{07}: There is no significant relationship between the size of the farm holding and the motive 'influenced by success stories'.

H_{17}: There is a significant relationship between the size of the farm holding and the motive 'influenced by success stories'.

H_{08}: There is no significant relationship between the size of the farm holding and the motive 'to gain employment'.

H_{18}: There is a significant relationship between the size of the farm holding and the motive 'to gain employment'.

H_{09}: There is no significant relationship between the size of the farm holding and the motive 'to gain social prestige'

H_{19}: There is a significant relationship between the size of the farm holding and the motive 'to gain social prestige'.

H_{010}: There is no significant relationship between the size of the farm holding and the motive 'to make use of idle funds'

H_{110}: There is a significant relationship between the size of the farm holding and the motive 'to make use of idle funds'

4.5. Tools Applied for Data Analysis

Simple statistical devices such as percentages and averages wherever relevant were used to interpret and analyse data collected. Factors motivating and facilitating entrepreneurship were rated by weighted scores.The data collected was also analysed by using statistical tools called SPSS. Kruskal-Wallis test was used to find whether there was any significant relationship between the motivation factors among the different group of farmers.

4.6. Limitations of the study

Some of the significant limitations are mentioned hereunder:

1. This study is limited to certain significant key aspects of entrepreneurship.
2. The study is restricted to examine the relationship between land holding and motivational factors.

Chapterisation

I. Introduction

II. The Present Study

III. Socio-economic Profile of Agripreneurs in Saitual Cluster.

IV. Role of Cluster Development on Emergence of Agripreneurship in Saitual.

V. Motivational Factors for Agripreneurship in Saitual cluster

VI. Financial Performance of Sericulture Enterprises.

VII. Summary of findings and suggestions.

References

Acharya, J. (1993). *Sericulture and development*. Indian Publishers Distributors, Delhi.

Agarwal, A.K. (1999). Industry in Mizoram, in A. Banerjee and B. Kar (eds), Ahmedabad, India.

Amit, R., MacCrimmon, K.R., Zietsma, C., & Oesch, J.M. (2001). Does money matter: Wealth attainment as the motive for initiating growth-oriented technology ventures. *Journal of Business Venturing*, 16(2), 119–143.

Bairwa, S.l., Lakra, K., Kushwaha, S., Meena, L.K., & Kumar, P. (2014). Agripreneurship Development as a Tool to Upliftment of Agriculture. International Journal of Scientific and Research Publications, 4(3), 1-4.

Baruah, S.S. (2000). Women Entrepreneurs in North East- Role of Training in Creating and Sustaining Micro enterprises, in Prabath, S, V, V Patil, C Rani, R Shukla and Rao Gopala (eds). *Women Entrepreneurs in India: Challenges and Achievements*. NISIET, Indian Express Newspapers Ltd, Hyderabad.

Becattini, G. (1991). Italian Industrial Districts: Problem & Perspectives. *International Studies of Management and Organization*, 21(1), 83-90.

Berna, James, S.J. (1960). *Industrial Entrepreneurship in Madras State*, Asia Best, M. (1990). On the Clustering of Small Firms. *IDS Bulletin*, 23, 64-9.

Bird, B. (1988). Implementing entrepreneurial ideas: The case for intention. Academy of Management Review, 13(3), 442–453.

Brusco, S. (1982). The Emilian Model: Productive Decentralisation and Social Integration. *Cambridge Journal of Economics*, 6, 167-84.

Cantillon, R. (1755). *Essai sur la nature du commerce en general* (ed. H. Higgs) London: Macmillan (1931).

Carter, S. (1998). Portfolio entrepreneurship in the farm sector: Indigenous growth in rural area. *Entrepreneurship and Rural Development*, 10(1). 17-32.

Cassar, G. (2007). Money, money, money? A longitudinal investigation of entrepreneur career reasons, growth preferences and achieved growth. *Entrepreneurship and Regional Development*, 19(1), 89–107.

Cawthorne, P. (1995). Of Networks and Markets: The Rise and Rise of a South Indian Town, the Example of Tiruppur's Cotton Knitwear Industry. *World Development*, 23(1).

Cho, M.R. (1994). Weaving Flexibility: Large–Small Firm Relations, Flexibility and Regional Clusters in South Korea, in P.O. Pedersen, A. Sverisson and. van Dijk, M, P (Eds), F*lexible Specialization: The Dynamics of Small-scale Industry in the South*, London: Intermediate Technology, London

Cole, A. (1959). *Business Enterprise in Social Setting,* Cambridge, Mass., Harvard University Press, 1959.

Chandan, R., Mukherjee, R., & Ghosh, S. (2013). Sericulture as an Employment Generating Household Industry in West Bengal - A Study on its Current Problems & Prospects, MPRA Paper No. 43672, posted 9. January 2013. Retrieved from https://mpra.ub.uni-muenchen.de/43672/ .

Chandrashekar, R.R. (1990). Inome and employment genmeration in Sericulture Via-vis alternative crops in Hosut Taluk in Dharmapuri Distirct. University of Agricultural Sciences, Bangalore 1990, Page No.128.

Chowdhuri, R.S., Umasankar., Das, N.K., Sahu, P.K., & Majumdar, M.K. (2011). Studies on involvement of women and their contribution share in sericulture activities. *Journal of Crop and Weed, 7(2)*, 37-40.

Cluster Promotion Programme 2008-2012. (2012). Central Sericultural Research & Training Institure, Central Silk Boar, Ministry of Textiles, Govt. of India.

Das, B. (2000). Emerging Trends In Women Entrepreneurship: A Study Of Kamrup District Of Assam, in Prabath, S, V; Patil V,C Rani, Shukla ,R; Rao Gopala;(eds). *Women Entrepreneurs in India: Challenges and Achievement*s, NISIET, Indian Express Newspapers Ltd, Hyderabad, pp. 172-186.

Das, K. (1995). Industrial Clustering in Developing Countries. *Productivity (Special Issue on Small Scale Sector)*, 36(1).

Das, K. (1999). Flexibility, Collectivity and Labour: Contextualizing the Industrial Cluster Debate in India. *The Indian Journal of Labour Economics.*

Das, K. (2003). *Competition and Response in Small Firm Clusters: Two Cases from Western India*, Gujarat Institute of Development Research, Ahmedabad, India, working paper no.142.

Das, K. (2005). *Industrial clusters in India: Perspectives and Issues for Research*, Working

Paper No. 159, Gujarat Institute of Development Research, Gota,Differences between Entrepreneurs and Managers", *Journal of Small Business Management*, Vol. 47, No. 4, pp 401-421.

Dewangan, S.K. (2017). Sericulture play key role to employment generation and socio-economic empowerment of tribal women. *International Journal of Advanced Research and Development*, 2(6), 761-768.

Diana, M.H., Maija, R., & Charles, H.M. (2012). The nascent entrepreneurship hub: goals, entrepreneurial self-efficacy and start-up outcomes.

Directorate of Sericulture: Aizawl, Mizoram. (2012). *Sericulture at a glance*, Information and Publicity Cell, Government of Mizoram.

Dollinger, M.J. (1995). Entrepreneurship Strategies and Resources, Irwin, Homewood.

Drucker, P.F. (1985). *Innovation and Entrepreneurship*, Oxford: Butterworth Heinemann, 1985.

Elwee, G. (2007). Important trends and required skills in Englang (UK). In Pieter de Wolf and Schoorleemer (Ed.). Exploring the Significance of Entrepreneurship in Agriculture, FiBL Publishers, and Switzerland, (2007), 18-28.

Gaikwad, V.R., & Tripathi, R.N. (1970). *Socio- Psychological Factors Influencing Industrial entrepreneurship in Rural Areas,* National Institute of Community Development, Hyderabad.

Gangadhara, R.N. (1986). *Entrepreneurship and Growth of Enterprises in Industrial Estates*, Deep and Deep Publications Pvt. Ltd, New Delhi.

Gray, C. (2002). Entrepreneurship, resistance to change and growth in small firms. *Journal of Small Business and Enterprises Development*, 9(1), 61-72.

Garg, R.B.L. (1979). Sericulture industry- The challenges ahead. Agricultural banker, 11(4), 7-10.

Government of Mizoram. (2011). *Mizoram Remote Sensing Application Centre (MIRSAC)*, Science & Technology, Planning Department, Government of Mizoram.

Hessels, J., Gelderen, M.V., & Thurik, R. (2008). Entrepreneurial aspirations, motivations and drivers. Small Business Econ, Vol. 31, Sept. 2008, 323-339.

Higgins, R. (1998). Local Business Co-operation, Training and Enterprise Councils: The Development of Inter-firm Networks. *Regional Studies*, 32(9), 813-826.

Holmstrom, M.M. (1993). A New Direction for Indian Industry? Bangalore as an Industrial District, *Report to the Overseas Development Administration*, School of Development Studies, University of East Anglia, Norwich, mimeo.

Hundal, P.S. (1977). *Entrepreneurial Motivation and its Structure*, ICSSR, New Delhi. Indian Institute of Entrepreneurship. (2005). *Evaluation cum Impact Study of STEP Project for Handloom Weavers of Assa'*, Indian Institute of Entrepreneurship, Guwahati.

Kabra, K.C. (2008). *Economic Growth of Mizoram- Role of Business and Industry*, Concept Publishing House, New Delhi.

Kashyap. S.P. (1992). *Recent Developments in the Small Enterprises Sector in India: Economic and Social Aspects'*, Discussion Paper No. 48, International Institute of Labour Studies, ILO, Geneva.

Kasi, E. (2013). Role of women in sericulture and community development: A study from a south Indian village. *SAGE*, 3(3), 1-11. Retrieved from http://sgo.sagepub.com/content /3/3/2158244013502984.

Khanka, S.S. (1990). *Entrepreneurship in Small-Scale Industries*, Himalaya Publishing, New Delhi.

Khanka, S.S. (2009). Motivational Orientation of Assamese Entrepreneurs in the SME Sector, *Journal of Entrepreneurship*, 18(2), 209-218.

Knight, F.H. (1942). Profit and Entrepreneurial Functions. *The Tasks of Common History: Supplement to Journal of Economic History*, 2, 126-132.

Knorringa, P. (1998). Barriers to Flexible Specialization in Agra's Footwear Industry, in M. Holmstrom,M and P. Cadene (eds). *Decentralized Production in India, Industrial Districts, Flexible Specialization and Employment*, Sage Publications, 283–307, New Delhi.

Kolvereid, L. (1992). Growth aspirations among Norwegian entrepreneurs. *Journal of Business Venturing*, 7(3), 209–222.

Krishnaswami, D.N.S. (1986). Mulberry Cultivation in South India. Central Sericultural Research & Training Institute, Mysore, Published by: Shri V. Balasubramanian, IAS, Member-SecretarY Central Silk Board United Mansions No. 39, Bangalore.

Kumara, S.B.K.(1993). Mulberry for drylands of Karnataka. Indian Silk Central Silk Board, Bangalore 1992.XXXI (6), 5-10.

Laskar, B.I. (2010). *Industrialisation in Mizoram-Problems and Prospects*, NCBA, Delhi. Lianzela. (1994*). Economic Development of Mizoram*, Spectrum Publications, Guwahati.

Locke, E.A., & Latham, G. (1990). A theory of goal setting and task performance, Englewood Cliffs, New Jersey: Prentice Hall.

Mali, D.D. (2000). Women Entrepreneurs In North-East India- A Few Cases of Created Entrepreneurs, in Prabath, S, V, V Patil, C Rani, R Shukla and Rao Gopala (eds), *Women Entrepreneurs in India: Challenges and Achievement*s, NISIET, Indian Express Newspapers Ltd, Hyderabad, 89-97.

Manimala, J.M. (1999). *Entrepreneurial Policies and Strategies: the Innovator's Choice*, Sage Publications.

Marshall, A. (1907). Principles of Economics, Macmillan, London.

Marshall, A. (1919). *Industry and Trade*, Macmillan, London Publishers, New Delhi.

McClelland, D.C. (1961). *The Achieving Society*, Princeton, NJ, Van Nostrand.

Mitsui, I. (2003). Industrial Cluster Policies and Regional Development in the age of Globalisation – Eastern and Western approaches and their Differences, presented in 30th International Small Business Congresses, 22nd September, 2003.

Morris, M.H., Miyasaki, N.N., Watters, C.E., & Coombes, S.M. (2006). The dilemma of growth: Understanding venture size choices of women entrepreneurs. *Journal of Small Business Management,* 44(2), 221–244.

Murthy. (1978). Sericulture can generate employment" Indian Silk, Central Silk Board, Bangalore. 1978 vol. 28, Page no. 36.

Nadvi, K. (1995). The Export Competitiveness of Small Producers: the Surgical Instruments Cluster of Sialkot'. Pakistan, mimeo, Brighton: *Institute of Development Studies*, University of Sussex.

Nafziger, E., & Wayne. (1978). *Class, Caste and Entrepreneurship: A Study of Indian Industrialists*. The University Press of Hawaii, Honolulu.

Nagalakshmi, T., & Sudhakar, A. (2013). A case study of Dharmapuri farmers. International Journal of Science and Research, 2 (8), 208-214.

Narendran, K., & Ranganathan, T.T. (2015). Agripreneurship for Rural Youth. International Journal in Management and Social Science, 3(8), 245-251.

Ostwald, M., Jonsson, A., Wibeck, V., & Asplund, T. (2012). Mapping energy crop cultivation and identifying motivational factors among Swedish farmers, *Biomass & Bioenergy,* 50, 25-34.

Pal, S., & K, Sood. (2004). *Dynamics of Growth and Stagnation of Industrial Clusters in India: Emerging Issues and Policy Imperatives'*, Entrepreneurship Development Institute of India, Ahmedabad.

Parilli, M.D. (2007). Cluster Trajectories in Developing Countries: A Stage and Eclectic Approach Applied to Survival Clusters in Central America', in Pitelis, C; Sugden, R and Wilson, J, R (Eds), *Clusters and Globalisation: The Development of Urban and Regional Economies*, Edward Elgar, USA.

Piore, M.J., & Sabel, C.F. (1984). *The Second Industrial Divide - Possibilities for Prosperity*. USA: Basic Books.

Porter, M. (1990). *The Competitive Advantage of Nations*. London: Macmillan.

Porter, M. (1998). *On Competition*, Harvard Business Review Book. Publishing House, Bombay.

Priyadarshini, M.B., & Kumari, N.V. (2013). A Study on the knowledge and adoption level of improved sericulture practices by the farmers of Chittoor district. *International Journal of Agricultural Science and Research*, 3(2), 43-46.

Puera, J., P, Siiskonen., & Vesala K.M. (2012). Entrepreneurial identity among the rural small business owner managers in Finland: In rurality, rural policy and politics in Nordic-Scottish perspective, HW Tanvig (ed). Esbjerg: Danish Centre for Rural Research and Development. Working Paper 1/2012.

Ragjagopalan. (1980). Impact of sericulture on income and employment in rural areas in TamilNadu. *Indian Silk*, Central Silk Board, XVI (7), 7-15.

Rajapurohit, A.R., & Govindaraju, K.V. (1981). Employment and Income in Sericulture. *Shiny Publications*, Bangalore 1981. Page no. 225.

Ramarao. (1978). Employement potential of Sericulture Industry. *Indian Silk*, Central Silk Board, Bangalore. 1978, 17 (6), 67-71.

Ramswamy, R., & Kumar J. N.V.R. (2011). Impact of cluster on entrepreneurship in tribal artisan clusters: A case study of Thenzawl handloom cluster, Mizoram. *SEDME,* 38(2), 39-51.

Rani, G.S. (2006). Women in sericulture, Discovery Publishing House, New Delhi.

Rathnam, N.V., & Narasaiah, P.V. (2012). Sericulture Industry – A Boon for Rural Poor: Special Focus on Chittoor District of A.P. *SEDME* 39(3), 17-33.

Rathnam, N., Narasaiah, P.V., & Murthy, S.D. (2013). Current status of silk industry in India – An evaluation. *SEDME*, 40(4), 55-67.

Raymond, W., & Habiyaremye, A. (2013). Sericulture on thousand Hills: Reeling Rwanda out of poverty. Retrieved from ww.merit.unu.edu/MEIDE/papers/2013/Raymond_Habiyaremye.pdf.

Roy, C., Mukherjee, S., & Ghosh, S. (2012). *Sericulture as an employment generating household industry in West Bengal: A study on its current problems & prospects*. Munich Personal RePEc Archive Paper No. 43672. Retrieved from https://mpra.ub.uni-muenchen.de/43672/

Sathish, A.V. (1985). Infact of Diversification and Liberal Credit Policy on Income and Employment of Non-Viable farmers in Pithepuram block of East Godavari Dist (A.P.). *Indian Journal of Agricultural Economics,* 1985 XL, (3), 323-329.

Say, J.B. (1803). *A Treatise on Political Economy: or, the Production, Distribution and Consumption of Wealth*, New York: Augustus M. Kelley (1964).

Schmitz, H. (1995). Small Shoemakers and Fordist Giants: Tale of a Super cluster. *World Development*, 23(1), 9–28.

Schumpeter, J. (1934). *The theory of economic development*, Harvard University Press.

Sharma, K.L. (1975). *Entrepreneurial Performance in Role Perspective*, Abhinav Publications, New Delhi.

Singh, A.P. (2012). Strategies for developing agripreneurship among farming community in Uttar Pradesh. *Journal of Asia Entrepreneurship and Sustainability,* 8(1), 81102.

Srivastav, N., & Raj, S. (2007). Marketing Management and Entrepreneurship Development in a Tribal Dominated Economy: A Case Study of Small Scale Industries in East Khasi Hills District of Meghalaya. *The ICFAI Journal of Entrepreneurship Development*, Vol. No. 4, 28-47, December 28-47.

Tripathi, R., & Agarwal, S. (2015). Rural development through agripreneurship: a study of farmers in Uttar Pradesh. *Global Journal of Advanced Research*, 2(2), 534-542.

Townsend, S. (2013) He will not be beet-en: Farmer fights back at cheap imports. The Telegraph, 06/06/2013, p. 14. Retrieved from: https://epubs.scu.edu.au/cgi/viewcontent.cgi?article=1615&context=theses

UNIDO. (2001). Women Entrepreneurship Development in Selected African Countries, Working Paper No.7.

Vishakanta. (2018). Cost and Benefits of Sericulture Farmers of Ramanagaram District of Karnataka. *International Journal for Research in Applied Science & Engineering Technology*, 6(4).

Wayne, H., Stewart, Jr., & Philip, L. R. (2007). A Meta_ Analysis of Achievement Motivation. *The Journal of Entrepreneurship*, 18(2), 209–218.

Chapter - 3

Socio-economic Characteristics of Entrepreneurs

This chapter proposes to study the socioeconomic characteristics, viz age, gender, educational qualifications, family structure, family size, occupation, year of commencement of business, marital status, age-sex distribution etc. of the entrepreneurs in Saitual cluster.

1. Introduction

The socioeconomic milieu plays an important role in the emergence and development of entrepreneurs as they are embedded in socioeconomic systems. The socioeconomic factors such as caste, parental occupation, income and age mould the attitudes of entrepreneurs. Gangadhara Rao (1986) in his study on industrial estates in coastal Andhra observed that entrepreneurship is a socioeconomic phenomenon.

Sericulture industry in India is known to be inherently inclusive in nature. Sericulture industry is an excellent avenue for employment with various entrepreneurial opportunities. India lives in villages and Sericulture being an agro-based enterprise, plays a predominant role in shaping the economic destiny of the rural people and fits very well in the India's rural structure, where agriculture continues to be the main occupation. The pursuit of sericulture offers gainful employment not only for the rural masses but also for the educated youth in semi-urban and urban areas. Growth of sericulture will certainly lead to vibrant rural economy by creating income generating entrepreneurial opportunities enabling poverty reduction. The development of sericulture industry in India is a case in point. Sericulture is said to provide an excellent opportunity for socioeconomic progress in the context of a developing country like India, due to various reasons. First and foremost, sericulture is a highly labor-intensive industry. Excluding mori-culture (mulberry cultivation), which is a cottage industry, silkworm rearing itself generates 1.5 and 4.5 person-years of employment per year per hectare of mulberry garden, under rainfed and irrigated conditions, respectively. In India, sericulture is recognized as an instrument for social and economic transformation of agriculture and occupies an important place in the development plans of the country. Sericulture provides direct and indirect employment opportunities. Direct employment includes mulberry cultivation, leaf harvesting, silk worm rearing whereas indirect employment it provided in the process of reeling, twisting, weaving, printing and dying, finishing and silk waste processing, Gangopadhyay (2008). Around 60 lakh persons are engaged in various sericulture activities in the country. It is estimated that Sericulture can generate employment @ 11 man days per kg of rawsilk production (in on-farm and off-farm activities) throughout the year. This potential ispar-excellence and no other industry generates this kind of employment, specially in rural areas, hence, sericulture is used as a tool for rural reconstruction (Central Silk Board, 2018).

Over the years sericulture is playing a vital role in development of the rural economy of Mizoram, in terms of employment opportunities. Mizoram occupies the 17th place in respect of area under mulberry, cocoon and silk raw production in India during 2011-2012 (Rathnam, Narasaiah and Murthy, 2013). The economy of Saitual is basically agrarian in nature and the major agricultural crops grown were corn, sugarcane and vegetables. Sericulture has become an important occupation in recent years after the cluster started taking its shape in 2009. As mentioned earlier, Saitual has been identified as one among 10 sericulture clusters in Mizoram. The cluster is an ideal place for taking up sericulture activities with vast tracts of land under cultivation of mulberry leaves. A study of the socioeconomic milieu of Saitual Cluster may provide a clue to the emergence of entrepreneurship in such clusters in tribal areas.

2. Commencement of Business in Saitual

Table 3.1: Year of Commencement of Business

Year	*Frequency*	*Percentage*
1994-1998	3	1.7
1999-2003	11	6.1
2004-2008	27	15
2009-2014	137	76.1
2015-	2	1.1
Total	**180**	**100.00**

Source: Field Work.

The genesis of sericulture in Mizoram can be traced back to 1934. It has made rapid strides of progress especially during the last two decades. Over the years sericulture has played a vital role as a means of livelihood for many households in the state. As seen from table 3.1, in the present study the birth of sericulture units shows a slow yet steady progress. Saitual cluster started to take its form in 1994 with one farmer engaging in sericulture for commercial purposes. The period between 2009-14 witnessed the birth of maximum number of units (137 units). This period coincided with the launching of the 'Cluster area development project' including Saitual cluster as on 2011-2012 (Directorate of Sericulture, Government of Mizoram, 2012) along with the initiatives taken by the Government through the scheme New Land Use Policy (NLUP). New Land Use Policy (NLUP) initiated on 14th January, 2011.

The main aim of the NLUP was to develop suitable and permanent trades among the farmers of the state. The Policy also aimed at giving all the farmers self-sufficiency in rice, vegetables etc. and support them financially. The number of farmers covered under NLUP were 2096 and 2100 in 2011-45 and 2012-13 respectively. The farmers in Saitual were given rearing appliances and other required materials under the scheme. As part of NLUP rearing houses had been constructed for 826 farmers under convergence with NLUP fund during 2011-2012. It has been observed that an overwhelming number of farmers in Saitual sericulture cluster were also selected under the scheme of NLUP. Evidently Saitual is an "induced cluster" where entrepreneurship has emerged as an outcome of cluster development activities initiated by Government of Mizoram through NLUP and Cluster Area Development Project (CADP). The present study has explored the role of cluster processes and the motivational factors that spurred the agripreneurs to take up sericulture as an economic activity in the following chapter.

The status of sericulture is often dependent on the various schemes and projects implement there by the government in several South Indian states. Studies in Tamil Nadu and Andhra Pradesh have corroborated that sericulture could be an alternative source to improve the living condition of marginal and small land holders. Sericulture has been regarded as a promising strategy for developing backward regions (Kasi, 2011). Several schemes launched in the states of Karnataka, Tamil Nadu and Andhra Pradesh gave an impetus to the development of this sector in these states (Kasi, 2011).

3. Gender

Table 3.2: Gender of the Farmers

Gender	*Frequency*	*Percentage*
Male	137	76.1
Female	43	23.9
Total	**180**	**100.0**

Source: Field Work.

Sericulture is largely a village-based industry that provides employment to both skilled and unskilled labor (Lakshmanan and Jayram, 1998). All family members, irrespective of gender and age, can contribute to the success of sericulture and, in this sense; it can be considered a home-based industry. Sericulture is practiced in villages of India as a family-based occupation and thereby also provides women a major role to play with, in various activities of this household-industry. Being argro-based in nature sericulture provides job opportunities for males and females in a variety of activities involved (Rani, 2006). From the household, women are employed in sericulture operations, about 51% of women are assisting men in this lucrative industry to produce the "queen of textiles" (Kannan, 1987). Women were actively engaged in the mulberry fields for the removal of weeds and in leaf plucking. sericulture offers a vast scope to augment the family income in Saitual.

Table 3.2 shows that 76 percent of the farmers were males and 23.9 percent of females. In the present study, it seems that sericulture activity was more prevalent in households headed by male decision makers and most of the silk worm rearing houses were owned by male beneficiaries. The same trend was found in a case study done in Alomtola Village of Malda

4. Age of Agripreneurs

Table 3.3: Age of the Farmers

Age	*Frequency*	*Percentage*
Below 30	15	8.3
31-40	46	25.6
41-50	47	26.1
51-60	35	19.4
Above 60	37	20.6
Total	**180**	**100.0**

Source: Field Work.

District, West Bengal where the total family practicing sericulture (293), 151 were male and 142 were female. In another study, in the districts of Dhemaji and Lakimpur (Assam), out of the total sample of 1357 there were 614 (45 percent) male and 543 (40 percent) female practicing sericulture.

The distribution of population by different age groups as seen from the table reveals that out of the180 agripreneurs, a significant number of the farmers were in the age group of 41-50 years(47 percent), followed by the age group of 31-40 years(46 percent) and farmers who were above 60 years of age (37 percent). 35 percent of the farmer was in the age group of 51-60 and only 15 farmers (8.3 percent) were below 30 years of age. It is evident that there is no barrier of age in the activity and the different activities of sericulture is suitable for all age groups. As sericulture has proved as one of the economically viable occupations, farmers who are already experienced with others crops are highly interested in practicing this activity (Rani, 2006), which explains higher number of farmers in the cluster belonging to the older age group. The response among young sericulturists i.e. below 30 years is only 8.3 percent, it highlights the need of motivating younger generations towards this activity.

In a study conducted in Dharmapuri village in Andhra Pradesh, a similar trend was revealed where 60 percent of the total 100 respondents belong the age group of 31-40 years. 22 percent fall within the age group of 41-50, 16 percent of the agripreneurs age group is 25-30 years and remaining 2 percent respondents age group were above 51 years. Agripreneurs of Dharmapuri village were between the age group of 31-40. Another study done in Uttarakhand indicated that majority of the respondent women engaged in sericulture belonged to middle age group 21-41 with 73.50 percent followed by women above 41 years (14.16 percent) and young age group with 13.33 percent.

5. Tribal Framework of Agripreneurs

Table 3.4:The Distribution of Tribes/Sub -tribes/ Clans of Entrepreneurs

Sl. No.	*Tribe/Sub-Tribe/Clan*	*No. of Entrepren eurs*	*Percentage*
1.	Chhangte	17	9.44
2.	Chawngthu	12	6.67
3.	Chenkual	1	0.56
4.	Chhakchhuak	8	4.44
5.	Fanai	3	1.67

(Contd...)

6.	Hauhnar	6	3.33
7.	Hmar	9	5
8.	Hnamte	12	6.68
9.	Hrahsel	2	1.11
10.	Kawlni	5	3.78
11.	Khawlhring	15	8.33
12.	Khiangte	2	1.11
13.	Pachuau	19	10.56
14.	Ralte	14	7.78
15.	Renthlei	7	3.89
16.	Sailo	9	5
17.	Tlau bualchhuak	13	7.22
18.	Vanchhawng	11	6.11
19.	Varte	8	4.44
20.	Zadeng	7	3.89
	Total	**180**	**100.00**

Source: Field Work.

Nadvi (2004) has observed that clusters are marked by a strong sense of common social identity. This is often based on shared norms or common notions of community that lie in ethnic, religious, regional or cultural identities which can in turn result in local *social capita.*[1] Another unique feature of the Mizo society is the concept of '*tlawmngaihna*', which permeates the whole community and binds them together. The Mizo society is founded on this principle which continues to have wide acceptance in their society.

All the respondents were Mizos (*Assam–Burman sub-groups*[2] of the Tibeto Chinese race). It was also observed that none of the farmers belonged to the neighbouring country, Myanmar as is commonly observed in other parts of Mizoram such as Aizawl and Lunglei. All the respondents belonged to the ST category.

The Mizos are comprised of different tribes, sub tribes and clans. The state of Mizoram is inhabited by a number of tribes which may be broadly divided into nine major and thirteen minor tribes and sub- tribes (Verghese and Thanzawna 1997). These tribes and sub-tribes are further divided into a number of clans. The major tribes of Mizoram are:

> Lusei or Lutsei (consists of ten clans and six chief's clans), *Pawi* or *Lai,Hmar, Lakher* or *Mara, Paite* or *Vuite, Ralte* (sub tribe), *Chakma* or *Tsak* or *Sak*, *Riang* or *Tuikuk*, and *Mogh* or *Mok* or *Thakma*.The sub tribes are: *Chawngthu, Chawthe, Ngente, Khawlhring, Khiangte, Pautu,*

Rawite, Renthlei, Tlau, Vangchhia, Zawngte, Pang and *Bawng*. The *Lusei* consists of ten commoners and six chief's clans. The commoner's clans include *Pachuau, Chhangte*, *Chawngte, Hauhnar, Chuango, Chuaungo, Hrahsel, Tochhawng*, Vanchhawng and *Chhakchhuak*. The six Chief's clans include *Zadeng, Palian, Thangluah, Rivung, Rokhum* and *Sailo*.

As shown in the table 4, twenty different tribes or sub-tribes or clans were involved in the commercial production of cocoon in the cluster. Interestingly, only about 9 percent of the sample entrepreneurs belonged to the commoner's clans namely, *Zadeng* and *Sailo*. *Pachuau* were the largest tribe among the sample entrepreneurs (10.56 percent), followed by Chhangte (Commoner's clan) and Khawlhring (sub tribe) of the *Lusei* tribe.

It is observed that the sample entrepreneurs in Saitual cluster share a strong sense of common identity despite the fact that they belonged to different tribes or sub-tribes or clans and abound in 'social capital.'

Moreover, social relationships are not dominated by tribes or sub-tribes or clans within the Mizo community. This phenomenon seems to be unique to this cluster as it is evident from research literaturethat in other parts of India such as Uttarakhand and Karnataka the sericulture activities belonged predominantly to certain castes. The finding of the study done in Assam reveals that all the castes are involved in silk activities in the study area though Ahom caste dominates taking up all the silk activities. 'Mishing' community prefer eri rearing though a few rearers are involved in muga rearing with very few in all muga activities. Brahmin and Kalita castes also are in muga rearing but very few of them take up all the activities of muga and eri activities. Meanwhile, Kasi witnessed caste discrimination among the famers in a study conducted in Kotha Indlu village. The sericulture village of Kotha Indlu is a village with multiple castes.Under the Adarana Programme, the Department of Sericulture provided bamboo stands (*chandrikas*) to sericulturists who come under this scheme. Four sericulture farmers also got pesticides under this scheme in Kotha Indlu. However, they complained that sericulture officials are not properly distributing these pesticides to needy sericulturists. Since the village is numerically populated with members of the Balija castes, officials from the sericulture department favour these upper caste people while disbursing the schemes and other benefi ts, neglecting the lower castes sericulturists.

A glimpse into the classification of farm holdings shows that the size for mulberry land holdings in the study area varies from 0.5 acres to 3 acres. The farm holdings are classified into three categories viz., less than one acre, one to acres and more than two acres for analyzing the variables that influences sericulture activity. As indicated in the table 1.4, majority of land holdings are between one and two cares in the cluster.

6. Ownership of Land

Table 3.5: Categorisation of sample farmers according to their mulberry land holdings.

Land holding of Agripreneurs	*No. of farmers*	*Percentage*
Upto 1 acre	40	23.22
1 to 2 acres	86	47.8
Above 2 acres	54	30
Total	**180**	**100**

Source: Field Work.

It is clear from Table 3.5 that there are 23.22 percent of farmers practicing sericulture in the category of less than one acre and 47.8 percent farmers in the category one to two acres and around 30 percent farmers in the category of above two acres.

The sericulture enterprise is characterized by low investment and as such small and marginal farmers dominate the enterprise. These farmers maintain an average mulberry garden of one or two acres. Ample labour and a small land-base encourage the farmers to practise sericulture as a subsidiary occupation to agriculture. While income from crop production is seasonal, sericulture provides year-round income, which is an important incentive for the small farmers to take-up sericulture (Banerjee, 1994).

The classification of farmers based on the size of their landholdings differs among researchers from place to place. Rani (2006) classified farmers as small, medium and large farmers when the landholding is upto 1 acre, 1 to two acres and more than 2 acres respectively in Andhra Pradesh. P. Kumaresan et al (2008) did a study on large scale farmers in Coimbatore district of Tamil Nadu where mulberry farm size of more than or equal to five acres was considered as large scale farmers, farmer's land holdings were classified as Above 10 acres, 7.5 acres – 10 acres, 5.0 acres to 7.5 acres and less than 5 acres.

7. Educational Qualifications

Table 3.6: Educational Qualifications

Qualification	*Frequency*	*Percentage*
Illiterate	8	4.5
School	162	90.0
College	10	5.5
Total	**180**	**100.0**

Source: Field Work.

Education is an important factor which influences the status of farmers. The literacy of Saitual cluster is marginally lower than the literacy rate of Saitual town i.e 97.35 percent (Census, 2011) which is higher than the state average of 91.33 percent. In Saitual, Male literacy is around 97.37 % while female literacy rate is 97.33 % as per Census India 2011. There was one college Saitual College affiliated to Mizoram University (a central university) and several schools.

Table 3.6 shows the picture of the educational status of the farmers in the cluster. It is clear from the table that majority of farmers i.e. 162 (90 percent) in Saitual cluster were educated up to school level and only 10 farmers (5.6 percent) have collegiate education. There were 8 farmers who are illiterate. It also suggests that the the Saitual sericulture cluster scored favourably in the literacy rate. However, it emerged from the above analysis that entrepreneurship is not highly associated with the educational status of the individual.

8. Marital Status of Agripreneurs

Table 3.7: Marital Status

	Frequency	*Percentage*
Unmarried	11	6.1
Married	152	84.4
Divorced	5	3.8
Widowed	12	6.7
Total	**180**	**100.0**

Souce: Field Work.

Similarly, farmers practicing sericulture in Uttarakhand are also not highly educated where fifty percent of the respondents were having primary education followed by illiterate (30%) and high school (20%). None of the respondents had education up to intermediate or graduation and above.

Anna (1990) found that 49.02 percent of women entrepreneurs started their own unit between 26-35 years and majority (44.12%) of them was having matriculation as their highest qualification. Similar trend was also found among the farmers of Chittoor district of Andhra Pradesh where 6.6% of the respondents were higher educated, 35.5% respondents were up to secondary level. 33.2% respondents were primary educated and the remaining 25.5% farmers were illiterate.

The marital status of the entrepreneurs has been enquired to understand the support and encouragement provided by the family to the entrepreneur. It is observed that 84.4 percent of the sample entrepreneurs were married and 6.1 percent of the entrepreneurs were unmarried. This implies that married people were more involved in sericulture than other categories of different marital status. That could be attributed to the fact that sericulture being a family oriented occupation, gives scope for married men and women and also large families. Similarly, in Uttarakhand majority of the respondents were married 79.16% followed by unmarried 14.16%. Very few percentages of the respondents come under the category of widow and divorcee (5.00% and 1.66%) respectively.

9. Caste

Table 3.8: Community/Tribe

Tribe	*Frequency*	*Percentage*
ST	180	100.0
SC	0	.0
OBC	0	.6
Others	0	.0
Total	**180**	**100.0**

Source: Field Work.

It is clear from table 3.8 that all the farmers belong to Scheduled Tribe (ST) in Saitual and all belonged to the Mizo community. In India the social stratification in rural communities is generally based on caste distribution. It is evident that in Saitual cluster such type of stratification based on caste does not find a place. However, the same cannot be said about the other states. In Uttarakhand the caste distribution of the women engaged in Sericulture activities according to caste classification showed that 57 respondents (47.50%) belonged to other backward caste (which included Muslims, Ahirs) followed by Scheduled caste (38.33%), which included Gorkhaali, and Jatav. Only 1.16 percent of respondents belonged to general category which included Rajputs and Thakurs. An analytical perusal of data revealed that respondents of all the selected villages were highly associated with the membership of Other Backward Caste and Scheduled Caste. Some social factors which accounted for the ascendancy of lower caste in the sphere of sericulture enterprise that might be because of traditional power inherited to them maximum exposure to the work of that particular enterprise, low earning and labour intensive business.

Another reason for lower caste women adopting sericulture as an enterprise was that they were socio economically downtrodden and it provided additional income for their livelihood. They were prefect to earn bread adopting this enterprise rather than through education and status and hence they have considerable strength performing in the Sericulture enterprise. Rani G.S (2006) found that 240 sample farmers 64 belong to scheduled castes (SC) five belong to Scheduled Tribes (STs), 63 belong to Backward Castes (BCs) and 10 farmers belong to other castes (OCs). It is interesting to observe that in all the four districts the percentage of farmers belong to other castes is high (45 percent).

10. Religion

Table 3.9: Religion

Religion	*Frequency*	*Percentage*
Christian	180	100
Others	-	-
Total	**180**	**100**

Source: Field Work.

As the majority (87%) of Mizos are Christians in various denominations, interestingly all the farmers in the Saitual cluster were Christians. However, studies revealed that religion does not influence the practice of sericulture as it can be witnessed from other states namely Murshidabad and Malda of West Bengal where most of the farmers' practice sericulture and in the non-traditional sericultural states namely Meghalaya and Tripura. About 45% of the total respondents belong to Muslim, 30% Hindu & 25% in Christian communities with 70% Muslim & 30% Hindu in Murshidabad; 90% Muslim & 10% Hindu in Maida; 100% Christian in Meghalaya and 15% Muslim & 85% Hindu in Tripura. (Chowdhury et. al, 2011)

11. Family Structure

Table 3.10: Family Structure

Family Structure	*Frequency*	*Percentage*
Living with parents	42	23.3
Lives separately	138	76.7
Total	**180**	**100.0**

Source: Field Work.

Traditionally the Indian society followed the joint family system. However, it has been observed that as a consequence of growing industrialisation and urbanization, joint family system is slowly disintegrating, giving way to the independent family system. The sample entrepreneurs were asked whether their family was a nuclear family or a joint family. It is observed that a high proportion (76.7 percent) of the sample entrepreneurs in this cluster lives separately, this is because the maximum number of the farmers were in the age group of 41-50 years (47 percent) and were likely to be married with a family of their own. Only 23.3 percent of the entrepreneurs were still living with parents.

Similar trend was found in Anantapur, Chittoor, Kurnool and Cuddapath districts in Andhra Pradesh where out of 240 sample farmers 195 farmers are living in nuclear families which accounts to 81.2 percent, and 45 farmers are living in joint families (i.e 18.8 percent). This may be attributed to the impact of social transformation that is taking place in the society.

12. Size of Family

Table 3.11: Number of Family Members

Size of Family	*Frequency*	*Percentage*
Below 5	105	58.3
6-10	73	40.6
11-15	2	1.1
Total	**180**	**100.0**

Source: Field Work.

The adoption of a particular enterprise may be primary or secondary which depends upon the availability of family labour and likewise sericulture is no exception. In this backdrop information was generated to segregate the sample households as per size of family members and the statistics are depicted in Table 3.11. It can be gathered from the table that majority of the farmers i.e. 58.3 percent of the sample beneficiary households had family size below five members and followed by farmers belonging to 610 members of family (40.6 percent). It can be said that sericulture activity is not confined to those households who have large number of family members. So was in the case of Krishnagiri district (Tamil Nadu), where it was observed that most of the small size family holders (89.7%) are involved in sericulture when compared with big (6.9%) and single family holders (3.4%). Small family holders are acting as economic group when compared with high (6.90%) and marginal (10.3%) economic groups. However, in Uttarakhand sericulture activity is practiced the mostly where the family size is large.

The data pertaining to the family size of the respondents were collected under three categories viz. small (1-4 members), medium (4-6 members) and large (more than 6 members), which reflected that most of the respondents (45%) belonged to large family size followed by medium(44.16%) and small family size (10.84%). The reason of this type of findings can be expressed as in case of the large family size, attention is more diverted towards earning the bread and butter for the family rather than giving importance to other public welfare activities. To conclude it can be said that sericulture activity is equally prevalent in households with small and large number of family members.

13. Native Origin

Table 3.12: Migration

	Frequency	*Percentage*
Yes	69	38.3
No	111	61.7
Total	**180**	**100.0**

Source: Field Work.

Table 3.13: Reason for Migration

	Frequency	*Percentage*
Employment	44	74.58
Marriage	6	10.17
Others	6	10.17
No response	3	5.08
Total	**59**	**100.00**

Source: Field Work.

Most of the entrepreneurs (61.7 percent) were natives of Saitual. Around 38.3 percent of the respondents have migrated to Saitual town from other places in Mizoram.

Table 3.12 further shows the different reasons which led them to their migration.

Out of the total entrepreneurs who have migrated from other places in Mizoram to Saitual town, a majority of 44 farmers have migrated in search of better opportunities for employment. Porter (1998) has observed that the existence of a cluster itself signals an opportunity. While local entrepreneurs are likely entrants to a cluster, entrepreneurs based outside a cluster frequently relocate, sooner or later, to a cluster location. It seems that the cluster dynamics has played a vital role in attracting entrepreneurs from other places in Mizoram to Saitual in search of employment opportunities.

14. Main Source of Income

Sericulture is practiced in about 52,360 villages all over the country and provides employment to about 7.56 million people, most of them being small and marginal farmers in rural areas, creating employment to at least for 12-13 people per hectare of mulberry. India is earning more than Rs 3,000 crore rupees from export of silk fabrics, waste and garments (Bharathi.D, 2016). In addition to high export opportunities, silk is having very good domestic market and strong handloom base blended with artisan skill, which is the real strength of the Indian sericulture industry. Sericulture being an agro-based enterprise plays a predominant role in shaping the economic destiny of the rural people. It holds promise as an employment generating industry, especially in rural and semi-urban areas. Several socio-economic studies have affirmed that the benefit-cost ratio in sericulture is highest among comparable agricultural crops.

3.14: Cost: Benefit analysis of mulberry sericulture and other competing crops.

Item	*Mulberry sericulture*	*Sugarcane*	*Turmeric*
Total input costs	48,659	30,575	29,610
Gross returns	96,132	60,200	55,317
Net returns	47,476	29,625	25,707
Crop period	1 year	1 year	4-5 months

Source: Dandin et al. presented at the 20th Conference of the international Sericulture. Commision, Bangalore, December, 2005.

Sericulture activity being subsidiary/secondary in nature, it is because of fluctuation that are taking place very frequently in the cocoon yield and their prices and to some extent the involvement of skilled labourers in certain activities (Rani G.S,2006).

The study attempted to know the main occupation of the sample entrepreneurs' family in order to find out the number of entrepreneurs solely dependent on sericulture. Table 3.15 shows the main occupation of the entrepreneur's family. In the chapters to follow, the researcher has estimated the economics of sericulture in Saitual and the returns that accrue to the agripreneurs.

Table 3.15: Main Source of Income

Source of Income	*Frequency*	*Percentage*
Sericulture	149	77.3
Business	16	8.9
Government's Job	11	6.1
Others	14	7.8
Total	**180**	**100.0**

Source: Field Work.

It is observed that 77.3 percent of the entrepreneurs were solely dependent on sericulture. Only 8.9 percent entrepreneur's considered business as their main occupation and for 11 entrepreneurs, Government's job was the main occupation. Sericulture has emerged as the main occupation of the agripreneurs in Saitual cluster. Kurumpatti Cluster provides of poorer people with sericulture as the main source of livelihood. Out of 193 households, there are 86 households doing sericulture, a majority of them belonging to the marginal and small categories of farmers. Muthurampatti Cluster predominantly consists of marginal and small farmers. Only about 13% of the households are sericulturists and a majority of them are marginal and small farmers.

14.1 Income of Entrepreneurs from all Sources

The income earned from all sources (including sericulture) for the entrepreneurs' families was also enquired into to find out the levels of dependence of the entrepreneurs on sericulture as a source of income.

Table 3.16 shows the average annual earnings of the entrepreneurs in Saitual cluster from all sources including sericulture. As observed in Table 3.15, 77 percent of the entrepreneurs are solely dependent on sericulture

Table 3.16: Annual Income from All Sources

Income	*Frequency*	*Percentage*
Below Rs,50,000	7	3.89
50,000-1,00,000	10	5.56
1,00,000-1,50,000	48	26.67
1,50,000-2,00,000	53	29.44
Above 2,00,000	62	34.44
Total	**180**	**100**

Source: Field Work.

for their livelihood. The income of the others is supplemented by trade and other economic activities. It is observed from Table 1.16 that majority of the farmers (34 %) earn above Rs.2,00,000 and 53 farmers (29 %) earn between Rs.1,50,00 – Rs. 2,00,000 and around 27 percent of the farmers earn between Rs.1,00,000 and Rs.1,50,000. Only 17 farmers earn below Rs.1, 00,000.

14.2 Income from Enterprise

Income from a given activity is a strong stimulant to the growth and development of entrepreneurship in that sphere. Profit is an important determinant of success for any enterprise and a motivating factor for others to enter the same line of business. It is also important for the substenance and growth of an enterprise.

Table 3.17: Annual Income from Sericulture

Income	*Frequency*	*Percentage*
Below Rs,50,000	20	11.11
50,000-1,00,000	20	11.11
1,00,000-1,50,000	40	23.22
1,50,000-2,00,000	46	25.56
Above 2,00,000	54	30
Total	**180**	**100**

Source: Field Work.

Table 3.17 shows the annual average income of the entrepreneurs from sericulture activities.

It is evident that majority of the farmers (30 percent) earn above Rs.2, 00,000 annually solely from sericulture activity. Interestingly, the number of large farmers in Saitual cluster are 54 (Table 3.5) with land holding of above 2 acres. It is clear that the large farmers of the cluster are the ones earning above Rs. 2, 00,000. Around 26 percent (46) of the farmers earn between Rs.1, 50,000 to Rs. 2,00,000 and around 22 percent (40) of the farmers earn Rs.100,000 to Rs.1,50,000. The remaining 40 farmers (22 percent) earn below Rs. 1,00,000.

15. CONCLUSION

Sericulture has emerged as a sustainable livelihood option for the farmers of Saitual cluster. The cluster has made significant strides in number of enterprises since 2009 which has coincided with the cluster development initiatives undertaken by the Government of Mizoram towards developing sericulture in the state.

Perceptibly, the cluster development initiatives have played an important role in the emergence of entrepreneurship in Saitual. The cluster abounds with social capital as the agripreneurs are bound by religion, clan and community. The women comprised about 23 % (43 No.) in the cluster.

Notably, a huge majority (77.3 %) of the agripreneurs were dependent on Sericulture as their main occupation. The agripreneurs also derived remarkable returns from sericulture with majority of the farmers (30 percent) earning above Rs. 2,00,000 annually followed by 26 percent (46) of the farmers earning between Rs. 1, 50,000 to Rs. 2,00,000 and around 22 percent (40) of the farmers earning Rs. 100,000 to Rs. 1,50,000 annually.

References

Anna, V. (1990). Socio Economic Basis on Women Entrepreneurship. SEDME, 17(1), 17-47.

Banerjee, A. (1994). Dairying systems in India. *Indian Dairyman*, 46, 229-23.

Bharathi, D. (2016). Sericulture Industry in India – A Source of Employment Generation. *International Journal of Advanced Engineering Research and Science* (IJAERS), 3(10), 144-147.

Chowdhuri, R.S., Umasankar., Das, N.K,, Sahu, P.K., Majumdar, M.K. (2011). Studies on involvement of women and their contribution share in sericulture activities. *Journal of Crop and Weed*, 7(2), 37-40.

Central Silk Board. (2018). Retrieved from http://csb.gov.in/silk-sericulture/sericulture/.

Gangopadhyay. (2008). Silk Industry in India- A Review, Indian Science & Technology, NISTDS, CSIR, New Delhi.

Gangadhara, R.N. (1986). *Entrepreneurship and Growth of Enterprises in Industrial Estates*, Deep and Deep Publications Pvt. Ltd, New Delhi.

Government of Mizoram. (2012). Sericulture at a Glance. Information and Publicity Cell. Directorate of Sericulture, Aizawl, Mizoram.

Government of Mizoram. (2014). *Economic Survey, 2013–14*. Planning & Programme Implementation Department.

Kumaresan, P., Geetha, D.R.G., Rajadurai, S., Selvaraju, N.G., & Jayaram H. (2008). Performance of Large Scale Farming in Sericulture – An Economic Analysis. *Indian. J Agri. Econ,* 63(4).

Kasi E. (2011). Developmental Initiatives and Sericulture in a South Indian Village. SAGE 31(3), 213-229.

Lakshmanan, S., & Jayram, H. (1998). Manpower utilization in mulberry sericulture: An empirical analysis. Manpower Journal, 33, 49-63.

Kannan, V.A. (1987). Women in Silk industry. *Indian Silk*, 26(5), 4-7.

Nadvi, K., & Barrientos, S. (2004). *Industrial Clusters and Poverty Reduction: towards a Methodology for Poverty Reduction and Social Impact Assessment of Cluster Development Initiatives,* UNIDO, Vienna. Retrieved from http://www.ids.ac.uk/ids/global/pdfs/SB&KN_UNIDO2004.pdf

Narasaiah, P.V., Rathnam, N.V., & Murthy, S.D. (2013). Current Status of Silk Industry in India- An Evaluation. Small Enterprises Development, Management & Extension (SEDME), 40(4).

Porter, M. (1998). Clusters and the New Economics of Competition. *Harvard Business Review*, 76(6), 77–91.

Rani, G.S. (2006). Women in Sericulture, ISBN 81-81-8356-098-9, Discovery Publishing House, New Delhi.

Verghese, G., & Thanzawna, R.L. (1997). *A History of the Mizos Volume –I*, Vikas, New Delhi.

Chapter - 4

Role of Cluster Development on Emergence of Agripreneurship in Saitual

Entrepreneurship gives vitality to the economy and is a key element that fuels growth of economies. Literature suggests that clusters have a bearing on business creation (Marshall 1996, Krugman 1991; Rocha and Sternberg, 2005). Rocha (2004) further observed that research on the impact of clusters on entrepreneurship at the regional level is both theoretically and empirically limited due to conceptual, theoretical and methodological limitations. Although there is no dearth of research studies on different facets of cluster development and cluster processes, the researchers have not focused much on the relationship between clusters and entrepreneurship development in developing countries. Moreover, there is still less quantitative evidence on the role and impact of cluster-based economic policy, the case experience and the conceptual framework suggest some conclusions for policy makers. Clusters can improve the efficiency of economic policy tools and there are different ways to raise economic benefits from existing cluster (Ketels and Memedovic, 2008).

To this end, the present chapter intends to investigate the impact of cluster on entrepreneurship development. To achieve this objective, the researcher has attempted to assess the extent of influence exerted by the cluster on entrepreneurship in matters such as initial expectations of agripreneurs from support agencies, agripreneurs economic reasons for entering the sericulture industry and agripreneurs reasons for establishing their units in Saitual cluster.

1. Clusters and Entrepreneurship

Several studies suggest that clusters foster entrepreneurship by providing established relationships and better information about opportunities;

lowering entry and exit barriers; opening up niches of specialisation due to the low degree of vertical integration; promoting a competitive climate and strong rivalry among firms that impose pressure to innovate due to the presence of close competitors; providing role models, particularly local firms that have 'made it'; capturing important linkages, complementarities and spillovers from technology, skills, information and marketing; gathering information on the direction and pace of new business formation and innovation by analysing customer needs that cut across firms and industries; providing access to physical, financial and commercial infrastructure; easing the spin-offs of new companies from existing ones; reducing risk and uncertainty for aspiring entrepreneurs; and providing a cultural environment where establishing one's own business is normal and failure is not a social stigma (Pyke and Sengenberger 1992; Saxenian 1994; Rosenfeld 1997; OECD 1998; Porter 1990 as cited in Rocha 2004)

Clustering of firms sets into motion several advantages that create a spin-off of enterprises in the cluster. As observed by Nadvi and Barrientos (2004), clustering sets into motion of range of potential benefits which can be through externality gains, joint action, and local social capital. Clusters can set into motion processes that improve the ability of small firms to improve market across through externality gains through joint action. This can raise incomes for those who work in clusters, raise their assets and capabilities and have a significant impact on lowering levels of poverty and social deprivation.

These advantages have been spelt out by Michael E.Porter in his seminal study entitled 'Clusters and New Economics of Competition' (Porter, 1998). He defined clusters as 'geographic concentrations of interconnected companies, specialized suppliers, service providers, firms in related industries and associated institutions'. His works on clusters has fascinated scholars across the globe and have received larger attention in the academic literature Mills et al. (2008) observed that clusters enhance firm's access to specialized labour, materials, and equipment and enable in lowering the operating costs and entrepreneurship is one important means through which clusters achieve their benefits.

The present study has probed into the role of cluster in augmentation of entrepreneurship from the point of view of the agripreneurs. The study has attempted to understand whether clusters are fertile grounds for the emergence and development of entrepreneurship and how cluster have contributed to the development of entrepreneurship in Saitual cluster. Ramswamy and Jyoti Kumar (2011) enquired into the extent of influence exerted by cluster on the emergence of entrepreneurship in Thenzawl in matters of the initial expectations of entrepreneurs, the selection of the cluster for starting their units, alternate proposals in the absence of the cluster (through self-assessment).

The agripreneurs were asked to accord ranks to their reasons wherever needed in order of their importance. These reasons were subsequently rated by weighted score to recognize their underlying importance on the emergence of entrepreneurship in the cluster.

A choice of 'any other' was also provided to the agripreneurs so as to ensure that their choices were not limited to only the choices stated in the questionnaire. The first ranking factor reason carries three points, the second two points and the third one point. Hence, based on the percentage of the weighted score for each factor/reason, overall ranking has been arrived. Only the first three ranking have been taking into consideration and ranking beyond these has been discounted as not of much relevance. The researcher also attempted to examine the alternate proposals of the agripreneurs in the absence of the cluster.

The scope of the study is confined to the role played by Saitual cluster in the emergence and preservation of entrepreneurship. The extent of the influence exerted by the perceived advantages derived from cluster processes and cluster development initiatives on entrepreneurship in matters of the expectation of agripreneurs, the selection of the cluster for starting their units, alternate proposals in the absence of the cluster were enquired into.

2. Initial Expectations of Agripreneurs

The present study has identified the initial expectations of the agripreneurs at the time of commencement of their enterprise in Saitual cluster (Table 4.1). It is evident from Table 1 that availability of land was the dominant expectation of the agripreneurs at the time of starting their venture.

Table 4.1 reflects that 'utilization of available ;land for growing mulberry' of land has been accorded the highest rating of 33.06 percent followed by 'suitable climate' accorded second rank with a rating of 32.78 percent and 'assistance from government' has been assigned the third rank with a rating of 28.24 percent.

Entrepreneurship has sprung in Saitual cluster as an outcome of the primary expectation of utilizing land for sericulture activities. As observed in Table 4.1. Land is the most important requirement for practicing sericulture farming, for from it food for silkworms will be harvested. The agro-based sericulture begins with land related activities to grow silkworm.

Table 4.1: Initial Expectations of Agripreneurs

Factors	*Ranking of the Expectations*			*Weighted Score*	*Rating (%)*	*Rank*
	No. of Agripreneurs					
	Rank One	*Rank Two*	*Rank Three*			
Utilization of available land for growing mulberry.	78	48	27	357	33.06	1
Assistance from the state government or other agencies	38	65	61	305	28.24	3
Availability of dug wells, bore wells, canal and ponds for irrigation	-	7	30	44	4.07	4
Suitable climate condition for silkworm rearing.	64	60	42	354	32.78	2
Availability of skilled labour for farming activities.	-	-	20	20	1.85	5
Any other reason.	-	-	-	-	-	-
TOTAL	**180**	**180**	**180**	**1080**	**100**	

Source: Field Work.

Employment in sericulture primarily depends upon productivity of land as well as labour, and suitable climatic factors. The initial expectation 'utilization of available land for growing mulberry', implies land available to grow mulberry leaves that could be fed to the silkworm so as to produce silk. Silk is extracted from the cocoon of silk-worm which eats this mulberry leaf as its food.

Interestingly all the respondents in the present study owned land on which mulberry trees were grown and a majority of the farmers (70percent) were small farmers having land holding less than 2 acres, followed by medium farmers with land holding of 2 to 3 acres (26.11%) . Only 4.89 percent belonged to large farmers with land holding above 4 acres. This clearly emerged as the most significant factor that led the farmers to involve in sericulture where mulberry can be grown for silkworm rearing.

According to MIRSAC senior scientist Dr. Lalnunsiama Colney, "Mizoram has a large area of wasteland due to the destructive slash-and-burn or shifting cultivation where Mulberry and other trees can be successfully grown for silkworm rearing".

As mentioned earlier, Sericulture can be practiced even with very low land holding. Even three fourth of an acre of mulberry garden and silkworm rearing can support a family of three without hiring labour. Cases of landless families engaged in cocoon production using mulberry contracted from local farmers are common in some states. Ample labour and a small land-base encourage the farmers to practice sericulture as a subsidiary occupation to agriculture. While income from crop production is seasonal, sericulture provides year-round income, which is an important incentive for the small farmers to take-up sericulture (Banerjee, 1994).

In a place like West Bengal sericulture is a supplementary crop to the agriculture. Mostlysericulture is practiced by small land holder for their livelihood. West Bengal occupies about 53911 acres land under mulberry cultivation out of which, 26533 acres of land has been planted with High Yielding Verities (HYV) of mulberry. Sericulture is practiced in about 1625 villages and approximately 401000 people are employed for 13 persons per year. (Trivedi and Sarkar, 2015)

Suitable climatic condition has been accorded 2nd rank with an overall rating of 32.17 percent (Table 4.1). Climate is an important physical element which indicates the atmospheric conditions of heat, moisture and air circulation. It plays a dominant role in sericulture activities. Climate conditions influence the performance of sericulture, specifically the silkworm rearing depends largely on the moderate temperature and relative humidity. The success of sericulture depends to great extent on abiotic envoironmental conditions and temperature plays an important role on the growth and productivity of silkworms. The optimum temperature for normal growth of silkworms is between 20 degrees Celsius and 28 degrees celcius. (Rahmathulla, 2012)

The study area is having the climate condition and soil congenial to practice sericulture and it is evident that if plays a major role in successfully meeting the expectation of the farmers. Temperature plays a vital role on the growth of the silkworms. As silkworms are cold-blooded animals, temperature will have a direct effect on various physiological activities. In general, the early instar larvae are resistant to high temperature which also helps in improving survival rate and cocoon characters. The temperature has a direct correlation with the growth of silkworm; wide fluctuation of temperature is harmful to the development of silkworm. The combined effect of both temperature and humidity largely determines the satisfactory growth of the silkworms and production of goodquality cocoons. It directly influences the physiological functions of the silkworm. The young-age silkworms can withstand to high humidity conditions than later-age worms and under such condition, the growth of worm is vigorous (Rahmathulla, 2012). Moreover the soil of Mizoram is naturally suitable to grow a healthy mulberry garden without the help of fertilizers. Notably none of the agripreneurs were treating their land with fertilizers.

Mizoram state is known to enjoy a moderate and uniform climate all through the year. This enables the production of bivoltine silk cocoon. The state's climate is essentially well suited to the requirements of sericulture which is why it became one of the main factors that led to the practice of sericulture in the cluster.

Assistance from the government has played a crucial role in the formation of this cluster. It has emerged as the third important factor with 164 agripreneurs, having accorded the top three ranks to this factor with an overall rating of 28.24 percent.

According to Khandwall (1977) when initiatives are directed towards influencing enterprise creation by way of providing technological inputs, financial assistance, infrastructural facilities and so forth, this type of environment directly facilitates various tasks involved in enterprise creation. He alternatively referred to this environment as task environment or facilitative environment.

Enterprise support initiative in developing countries have often directed exclusively towards the facilitation of the task environment (Manimala *et al.*, 2009). They further observed that the process of creating a supportive environment for enterprise creation should be a two pronged process: (a) creating necessary changes in the general environment or formative environment and (b) introducing changes in the task or facilitative environment so as to channelize the initiatives of enterprising individuals into entrepreneurship. The various components of the task environment could be enterprise specific infrastructure, industrial estates/special economic zones, specific training/education programmes, access to finance or capital, subsidized power supply, technology transfer and commercialization of technology, raw material supply, marketing support and so on. There is a lack of understanding of the role of task facilitation in creating conducive environmental activities (Markley & Macke, 2003). However, it has emerged as a major tool used by the governments to enterprise creation (Manimala *et al.*, 2009).

In India, the status of sericulture in given areas is dependent on various local schemes and projects implemented by the government. Central Silk

Board came into existence during 1949 for the development of the silk industry in India, with the enactment of the Central Silk Board Act, 1948. The Central Silk Board, a statutory body, is functioning under the administrative control of the Ministry of Textiles, Govt. of India, with its Headquarters at Bangalore. The Board's activities include Research and Technology Development, Seed Maintenance, and Development of Sericulture and Silk

Industry through which it supports, supplement and facilitates the efforts of State Governments. The Board extends support, supplement and facilitates the efforts of State Governments. The Board extends support to the States in the form of joint projects and development assistance under the plan schemes. Saitual is an "induced cluster" where entrepreneurship has emerged as an outcome of cluster development activities initiated by Government of Mizoram through NLUP and Cluster area development project (CDP), one of the flagship schemes of Central Silk Board (CSB), Ministry of Textiles. The central silk Board proposed in XIIth plan to formulate 179 clusters all over India, including Mizoram.

The farmers in Saitual are receiving assistance from the Governemnt in the nature of assistance for the construction of separate rearing house and procurement of improved rearing equipments; timely supply of good quality disease free layings to the farmers; distribution of quality disinfectants to the farmers for successful harvest of cocoon crops without any disease attack in Silkworm rearing; marketing facilities for the sale of cocoons produced and so on.

It is evident from the table that the assistance the received from the government has played a crucial role in spurring the agripreneurs to opt for engaging in sericulture activities.

In a study conducted in Daramdin Rose cluster, Sikkim it was observed that assistance from state government or other agencies have been accorded the highest rank

(Chhetri, 2018). Gangadhara Rao (1986) in his study conducted on industrial estates in Coastal Andhra Pradesh, revealed that assistance from state agencies and allotment of plot shed were the most important expectations of entrepreneurs, and expectations from family members, friends and relatives was the least expectations from entrepreneurs. Conversely, in a study conducted in Thenzawl handloom cluster in Mizoram (Ramswamy and Jyoti Kumar, 2011), it was observed that the initial expectations of the entrepreneurs from the government agencies in the form of assistance played a negligible role in stimulating entrepreneurship in that cluster.

Interestingly, 'availability of dug wells, bore wells, canal and ponds for irrigation' and 'availability of skilled labour for farming activities' were not significant initial expectations of the agripreneurs, as the ratings were only 4.07 oercent and 1.85 percent respectively.

The fact that 'availability of dug wells, bore wells, canal and ponds for irrigation' was not a significant expectation may be attributed to the fact that Mizoram is endowed with adequate rainfall and the agripreneurs do not depend on irrigation facilities for growing mulberry in their farm. Indian agriculture is mainly classified into two categories on the basis of availability of water resources, namely, rain-fed or dry-land farming and irrigated farming. Indian agriculture remains primarily rain-dependent, and rain-fed agriculture supports roughly 40 percent of the total cultivated area, as many studies examine from different angles. India has a net sown area of over 140 million hectares, of which only 41.2 million hectares are under irrigation (Lakshmanan et al.,1998; Sati, 2008). Irrigation facilities are clearly inadequate in India, which often means that agriculture is largely a gamble at the mercy of the monsoons (Kasi, 2011). As mulberry is highly versatile in nature, it is cultivated in a variety of soil types, a wide range of agroclimatic conditions and in both rainfed and irrigated areas. Saitual cluster is bestowned upon with congenial climate for sericulture where all the farmers are rain-fed farmers.

It is evident from literature that sericulture farmers utilize their family members in the activity in most parts of the country (Roy & Sarkar; Roy et al 2012; Deshingkar and Farrington 2006, Lakshmanan and Devi 2007). Notably, the finding of the present study cooroborate existing literature. In Saitual also agripreneurs were dependendent of family members for the activity and did not have expectations of hiring labour for their sericulture activities.

3. Degree of Fulfilment of Agripreneurs Expectations

Further the present study also sought a self-assessment of the fulfilment of the agripreneurs initial expectations presented in Table 4.2.

It is evident from Table 4.2 that 66.67 percent of the agripreneurs seem to have achieved fulfilment of their expectations, where 17.77 percent of the agripreneurs expressed discontent with their initial expectations. This may be attributed to the fact that majority of the farmers are satisfied that land were available to each of them to grow mulberry garden in the cluster. Though the number of acres owned by each farmer may differ, sericulture can be practice even with a very low land holding.

Table 4.2: Degree of Fulfilment of Agripreneurs Expectations

Responses	*No. of Agripreneurs*	*Percentage*
Very Much Fulfilled	20	11.11
Fulfilled	100	55.56
Undecided (Neither Fulfilled nor Unfulfilled)	28	15.56
Partly Fulfilled	30	16.67
Not at all Fulfilled	2	1.10
Total	**180**	**100**

Source: Field Work.

Moreover, the farmers were largely satisfied with the government in terms of assistance extended to them. During the field survey, the researcher observed that the agripreneurs built their own rearing shed near their mulberry garden with the funds given to them by the government and also they were well equipped with the different equipments for silkworm rearing such as rearing beds, bed cleaning nets, mountages etc. which were provided by the government as well.

4. Agripreneurs Reasons for Entering Sericulture Industry

The present study has also attempted to examine the reasons behind the entry of agripreneurs into sericulture. It can be observed from table 4.3, that the highest rating was accorded to the reason, 'Easy to establish mulberry garden' (32.96 percent) followed by 'ownership of agriculture land' (28.80 percent) and 'involvement of family labour' (16.11%).

Table 4.3: Agripreneur's Reasons for Entering Sericulture Industry

Factors	*Ranking of the Expectations*			*Weighted Score*	*Rating (%)*	*Rank*
	No. of Agripreneurs					
	Rank One	*Rank Two*	*Rank Three*			
Easy to establish mulberry garden	62	62	46	356	32.96	1
Ownership of agriculture land	40	61	69	311	28.80	2
High margin of profit	-	-	16	16	1.48	6
No difficulty in sercuring Dfls/Seeds	17	21	25	118	10.93	7

(Contd...)

No difficulty in securing rearing equipments/applian ces	10	8	6	52	4.81	5
Existence of similar units in the cluster	11	6	8	53	4.91	4
Skill of farming/rearing	-	-	-	-	-	8
Involvement of family labour	40	22	10	174	16.11	3
Any other	-	-	-	-	-	-
TOTAL	**180**	**180**	**180**	**1080**	**100**	

Source: Field Work.

It is evident that 'easy to establish mulberry garden' has emerged as the most significant reason for the agriprineurs to start sericulture activities with 62 out of 180 of them having accorded 1st rank to this factor, followed by 62 having accorded 2nd rank and 46 having accorded the 3rd rank with an overall rating of 32.96 percent based on weighted score. Ownership of land has been accorded 2nd rank with 40 out of 180 of the agripreneurs accorded 1st rank to the factor.

Notably, land plays the most important factor for the agripreneurs in the cluster that led them to enter the sericulture industry. This agro-based ocupation begins with land related activities to grow silkworm where mulberry garden are grown first. Mulberry is a plant that is grown for silkworm rearing. It is the exclusive food for the silkworm, which during its larval life is reared for silk production. Mulberry forms the basic food material for silkworms. It is estimated that one metric ton of mulberry leaves is necessary for the rearing of silkworms emerging out of one case of eggs which will yield about 25 kg to 30 kg of cocoons of high quality (Tuigong DR., 2015). Mulberry plant can grow and thrive very well in Saitual due to suitable climate that are favourable for mulberry plant. Mulberry cultivation and silkworm rearing are conducted round year. It is usually observed that five to six crops can be cultivated from one acre of mulberry gardening every year. On the other hand, many agricultural crops like paddy, sugar cane, turmeric and banana are planted and harvested once in a year and therefore could provide limited employment opportunities compared to sericulture (Roy et al, 2012).

Involvement of family labour emerged as another significant reason for the agripreneurs to enter into sericulture industry with a rating of 16.11 percent. It has been accorded the highest ranking (1st rank) by 40 number of agripreneurs. The sericulture industry, being highly labour intensive, could be used as an effective tool to generating gainful employement to a large number of people. Labour is required in silk cocoon production for different operations such as cultivation of mulberry plants, harvesting of mulberry leaves, transporting of leaves from the garden to the rearing shed, feeding silk worms, cleaning bed placing the ripe silkworms on mountage and finally collecting the cocoons from mountages.

It was observed that the activities involved in cultivation and rearing have generated employment for the male and female family members in the cluster. However, for activities such as harvesting of leaves which requires skilled farmers some of the medium and large farmers have engaged hired labourers.

It is evident from literature that sericulture farmers utilize their family members in the activity in most parts of the country (Roy & Sarkar 2015; Roy et al 2012, Deshingkar and Farrington 2006, Lakshmanan and Devi 2007). Notably, the finding is in consonance with the finding in Table 4.1 where the agripreneurs were not having any initial expectations of hiring skilled labour in the cluster. This may be attributed to 'involvement of family labour' in the enterprise.

Sericulture is an agro based industry which provides a continuous income throughout the year. Sericulture serves as an important tool for rural reconstruction, benefiting the weaker sections of the society; sericulture provides not only periodical turn within short period of time but also assures own family employment opportunities around the year (Lakshmanan et al., 1998). Sericulture is essentially a village-based industry that provides employment to both skilled and unskilled labour. At present, it is estimated that every hectare of mulberry plants provides employment to more than 15 persons. All family members, irrespective of gender and age, can contribute to the success of sericulture and, it can be considered a home-based industry. Silkworm rearing and mulberry leaf growing are the initial components of work through which involvement of family workers and wage workers takes place. It has often been observed that the hectare of land cultivated for mulberry determine the level of raw silk production and hence it can be assumed as an influencing factor of level behind employment generation in sericulture.

According to a study undertaken in two districts of Tamil Nadu (Lakshman et. al., 2007) among the alternative crops sugarcane, turmeric, paddy, maize and vegetables were taken. It was inferred that among three annual crops (sericulture, turmeric, sugarcane), sericulture has the potential to create maximum employment opportunities. It generates highest mandays throughout the year, followed by sugarcane, paddy, maize and vegetable. It has also been estimated from that field study that of the 532 mandays, nearly 60% (i.e 319.2 mandays) had been drawn from family labour; the remaining 40% of the labour force were, on an average, hired. Thus household sector itself becomes a source as well as supplier of workforce. This particular nature of sericulture helps the economy to combat the rural poverty, which is also another inherent feature of this developing economy.

A study conducted in Maharashtra (Hazare, 2008) reveals that mulberry sericulture generates 170 man days, while alternative crop combinations like soybeanwheat, soybean-gram and cotto-pigeon pea generat 66, 61 and 65 mandays, respectively. A huge manpower is required for sericulture activities throughout the year and the sericulture farmers utilize their family members particularly the aged persons and women folk in it.

In West Bengal, 1.14 lakh families are occupied with sericulture activities in 2339 villages while Karnataka is the state with the largest number of families involved with sericulture. Andhra Pradesh and West Bengal are the close competitors so far numbers of family involvement is concerned. (Roy et al, 2012.) In a similar study conducted in daramdin Rose cluster, Sikkim, it was observed that government support emerged as the most significant economic reason for the agripreneurs to start floriculture activities (Chhetri, 2018).

5. Agripreneurs Reasons for Setting Up Enterprise

Table 4.4: Agripreneurs Reasons for Setting up Enterprise in Saitual Cluster

Factors	*Ranking of the Expectations*			*Weighted Score*	*Rating (%)*	*Rank*
	No. of Agripreneurs					
	Rank One	*Rank Two*	*Rank Three*			
Availability of land in the cluster	105	75	-	465	43.06	1
Availability of Dfls/Seeds	10	30	40	130	12.04	4
Nearness to cocoon collection centre	38	23	49	209	19.35	2
Availability of transport facilities	-	-	8	8	0.74	7
Existence of similar units in the cluster	-	-	3	3	0.28	8
Government support and assistance	27	20	32	153	14.17	3
Hometown or nearness to native place	-	22	20	64	5.93	5
Suitable climate condition	-	10	28	48	4.44	6
Availability of rearing shed	-	-	-	-	0.28	9
Any other reason	-	-	-	-	-	-
TOTAL	**180**	**180**	**180**	**1080**	**100**	

Source: Field Work.

The present study also enquired into the probable reasons behind the agripreneurs establishing his or her unit in the cluster to gain an insight into the role played by cluster processes on the emergence of entrepreneurship in Saitual.

Table 4.4 exhibits agripreneurs reason for setting up enterprise in Saitual cluster. Table 4.4 shows that the highest rating (1st rank) was accorded to availability of land in the cluster (43.06%), followed by nearness to cocoon purchasing centre having accorded the 2nd rank (19.35%) and government support and assistance was accorded the 3rd rank (14.17%). The findings in this table again corroborate with the findings in Table 4.1, where 'assistance from state government and other agencies' was one of the dominant initial expectations of the agripreneurs.

As discussed earlier, land plays a prominent role in development of sericulture business, the agro-based sericulture begins with land related activities to grow silkworm where mulberry garden are grown first. This factor has played a predominant role in the choice of the agripreneurs setting up their units in Saitual. All the farmers owns a land, there are no landless farmers in the cluster.

Further, 19.35 percent of the agripreneurs cited 'nearness to cocoon purchasing centre' as one of the reasons for setting up their enterprise in Saitual cluster. The farmers harvest the cocoon and bring the same to government-cocoon markets for selling their produce. The cocoon collection centre is the place set up by the government, it is that centre where all the farmers deliver their harvested cocoons for drying and weighing and then testing the cocoon for fixing the floor price based on the quality of the cocoon. It acts as middlemen between the farmers and the government. During the field study, the researche visited the purchasing centre, the farmers have been provided technical support by the Sericulture department by making available machines and equipments for drying and weighing the cocoons which were available in the centre.

The government had provided weighing scales[1], Cocoon drying Machines[2], Platform scale[3],Temparature Clock[4] ,Plastic trays – to put the cocoons and Room disinfectant in the Cocoon purchasing centre at Saitual sericulture cluster.

'Existence of similar units in the cluster' was ranked 4th with a rating of only 4.91 percent followed by other reasons.

6. Agripreneur's Proposal had There been no Cluster

The present study also enquired into the agripreneur's alternate proposals had there been no cluster in Saitual in order to gauge the magnitude of the desire for taking up any entrepreneurial ventures. The details are presented in Table 4.5.

Table 4.5: Agripreneurs Alternate Proposals

Sl. No.	*Alternate Plan*	*No. of Agripreneurs*	*Per Cent*
1.	Not to enter the same business	8	4.45
2.	To take up a job.	51	28.33
3.	To set up the same business elsewhere	24	14.33
4.	To start a different business	9	5
5.	Can't say	75	41.67
6.	To still take up sericulture	13	7.22
	Total	**180**	**100**

Source: Field Work.

As shown in Table 4.5, 75 (41.67%) agripreneurs out of 180 indicated that they were uncertain about their second opinion, as they cited 'can't say'. However, 51 (28.33%) of them would take up a new job while 24 (14.33%) of them will set up the same sericulture business elsewhere, this indicates that for these farmers the existence of a cluster influence their decision making regarding the location of their unit.

It is evident that the existence of cluster plays a huge role for some of the farmers as only 7.22 percent would like to take up sericulture had there been no cluster in Saitual meanwhile 8 percent of the agripreneurs indicated that they would not enter the same business.

7. Entrepreneurs Satisfaction Levelwith Common Facilities in the Cluster

Table 4.6: Entrepreneurs Satisfaction level with Common Facilities in the Cluster

Sl. No.	*Responses*	*No. of Agripreneurs*	*Percent*
1.	Very much satisfied	21	11.67
2.	Satisfied	83	46.11
3.	Undecided	19	10.56
4.	Not satisfied	51	28.33
5.	Not at all satisfied	6	4.33

Source: Field Work.

Table 4.6 exhibits the level of satisfaction of the farmers with the common facilities available to them in the cluster provided by the Sericulture department of Mizoram. As the table shows majority of the farmers i.e 104 farmers out of the 180 are satisfied with the facilities provided to them by the government. This may attribute to the fact that 'Cocoon purchasing centre' has been set up in the cluster where different facilities such as weighing scales, Cocoon drying Machines, Platform scale,Temparature Clock, Plastic trays – to put the cocoons and Room disinfectant. However, 57 of them are not satisfied by the facilities provided by the government in the cluster.

8. Conclusion

To sum up it is evident that availability of land and family labour complemented by suitable climate for sericulture along with assistance from the Government were key factors that spurred the agripreneurs to commence sericulture activities in Saitual cluster. Cluster development initiatives by the Government has played a key role in the emergence of entrepreneurship in the cluster. Cluster development activities initiated by the government as part of the CDP has been an overriding factor as compared to cluster processes in initiating farmers into sericulture in the cluster.

It is evident that the cluster is sustaining on the main plank of assistance offered by the government in the form of cocoon rearing house and facilities provided for sericulture in the cluster. Sericulture has emerged as a sustainable livelihood option in other parts of India and through sustained efforts by the government agenciessericulture as an economic activity has the potential to give high returns to the agripreneurs of Saitual cluster.

Notes

1. *Weighing scale*- is used to weigh the cocoons. The weight of the cocoons determine the quality of the cocoons. The higher the weight ,the higher is the rate for that cocoons.
2. *Cocoon drying Machine*- There are three Cocoon drying machines in the centre. One machine can dry 50 kgs of cocoons at one time.
3. *Platform scale*- is also used to weigh the cocoons. There is one platform scale available at the centre.
4. *Temperature Clock*- This device is used to measure the degree of temparature and humidity of the room.

References

Banerjee, A. (1994). Dairying systems in India. *Indian Dairyman*, *46*, 229–234. Retrieved from https://ageconsearch.umn.edu/bitstream/58416/2/G-Srinivasa.pdf

Benchamin, K. V., & Jolly, M. S. (1986). Principles of silkworm rearing. In S. Mahalingam (Ed.), *Proceedings of Seminar on Problems and Prospects of Sericulture* (pp. 63– 106). Central Sericultural Research & Training Institute, Mysore.

Chhetri, K. (2018). *Impact of cluster processes on entrepreneurship development: A study of Daramdin Rose Cluster, Sikkim* (Unpublished master's thesis). Aizawl: Department of Commerce, Mizoram University.

Datta, R. K. (1992). *Guidelines for bivoltine rearing*. Bangalore: Central Silk Board.

Deshingkar, P., & Farrington J. (2006). Rural labour markets in South Asia: Evidence from India and Bangladesh. *World Development Report*.

Eswarappa, K. (2011). Development initiatives and sericulture in a south Indian village. *South Asia Research*, *31*(3), 213–229.

Eswarappa, K. (2013). Role of women in sericulture and community development: A study from a south Indian village. *SAGE Open*. Retrieved from http://sgo.sagepub.com/content/3/3/2158244013502984.

Gangadhara, R. N. (1986). *Entrepreneurship and growth of enterprises in industrial estates*. New Delhi: Deep and Deep Publications Pvt Ltd.

Government of India. (2013). *Annual Report 2012–13*. Central Silk Board, Ministry of Textiles, Government of India, Bangalore.

Government of Mizoram. (2012). *Sericulture at a glance, information and publicity cell*. Aizawl: Directorate of Sericulture.

Government of Mizoram. (2014). *Economic Survey, 2013–14*. Planning & Programme Implementation Department.

Hazare, T. N. & Jadav. (2008). Sericulture Brings Better Income. *Indian Silk,* 46 (9)

Khandwalla, P. (1977). *The design of organizations*. New York, NY: Harcourt Brace Jovanovich.

Ketels, H. M., & Memedovic, O. (2008). From clusters to cluster-based economic development. *International Journal of Technological Learning, Innovation and Development*, *1*(3), 375–389.

Krishnaswami, S., Narasimhanna, S., Suryananrayana, S. K., & Kumarararaj, S. (1973). *Silkworm rearing:Sericulture Mannual-2*. Agricultural Services Bulletin. 15/2, FAO. Rome: United Nations Organization.

Lakhshmanan, S., & Geetha, D. (2007). Tamil Nadu—Employment Opportunities in Sericulture.*Indian Silk*,.*46*(7):18–20.

Lakshmanan, S., Mallikarjuna, B., Ganapathy, R. R., Jayaram, H., & Geetha, D. R. G. (1998). Studies on adoption of sericultural innovations at farmer's field in Tamil Nadu: An empirical analysis. *Indian Journal of Sericulture*, *37*(1), 52–56.

Manimala, M.J., Mitra, J., Singh, V. (2009). Enterprise support system: Nature and relevance. In Mathew J. Manimala, J. Mitra & V. Singh (Eds.), *Enterprise support system: An international perspective* (pp. 1–35). New Delhi: Response Books.

Markley, D., & Macke, D. (2003). Entrepreneurial support organizations. *The Centre for Rural Entrepreneurship*, Monograph, 6: 1–4.

Mills, K. G., Reynolds, E. B., & Reamer, A. (2008). *Clusters and competitiveness: A new federal role for stimulating regional economies*. Washington, DC: Brookings Institution Metropolitan Policy Programme.

Nadvi, K., & Barrientos, S. (2004). *Industrial clusters and poverty reduction—Towards a methodology for poverty and social impact assessment of cluster development initiatives*. Vienna: United Nations Industrial Development Organization.

Porter, M. E. (1998). Clusters and the new economics of competition. *Harvard Business Review*, *76*(6), 77–91. Retrieved from http://www.alanausterman.com/wpcontent/uploads/2009/12/Clusters-The-New-Economics-of-CompetitionMichael-Porter.pdf

Ramswamy, R., & Kumar, J. N. V. R. (2011). Impact of cluster on entrepreneurship in tribal artisan clusters: A case study of Thenzawl handloom cluster, Mizoram. *SEDME*, *38*(2), 39–51.

Rahmathulla,V.K. (2012). Management of Climatic Factors for Successful Silkworm (Bombyx mori L.) Crop and Higher Silk Production: A Review. *Hindawi Publishing Corporation, Psyche*. Retreieved from https://www.hindawi.com/journals/psyche/2012/121234/

Rathnam, N. V., & Narasaiah, P. V. (2012). Sericulture industry—A boon for rural poor: Special focus on Chittoor District of A.P. *SEDME*, *39*(3), 17–33.

Raymond, W., & Habiyaremye, A. (2013). *Sericulture on thousand hills: Reeling Rwanda out of poverty*. Retrieved from file:///C:/Users/Examxx/Downloads/Raymond_Habiyaremye%20(1).pdf Rocha, H. O. (2004). Entrepreneurship and development: The role of clusters. *Small Business Economics*, *23*(5), 363–400.

Rocha, H., & R, Sternberg. (2005). Entrepreneurship: The Role of Clusters Theoretical Perspectives and Empirical Evidence from Germany, *Small Business Economics*, 24, 3(02), 267-292.

Roy, C., Mukherjee, S., & Ghosh, S. (2012). *Sericulture as an employment generating household industry in West Bengal: A study on its current problems & prospects*. Munich Personal RePEc Archive Paper No. 43672. Retrieved from https://mpra.ub.uni-muenchen.de/43672/

Roy, P., & Sarkar, R. (2015). Work participation and income generation from sericulture: A case study of Alomtola village of Kaliachak-II block in Malda district, West Bengal. *Social and Economic Geography*, *1*(1), 31–36.

Trivedi, S., & Sarkar, K. (2015). Comparative study on income generation through agriculture crop and sericulture at farmer's level in Murshidabad district. *Journal of Entomology and Zoology Studies*, 3(1), 242-245.

Sati, V.P. (2008). Natural Resource Management and Food Security in the Alaknanda Basin of Garhwal Himalaya. *ENVIS Bulletin: Himalayan Ecology*, 16(2), 1–11.

Tuigong, DR., Kipkurgat, T.K., & Madars, D.S. (2015). Mulberry and Silk Production in Kenya, *Journal of Textile Science & Engineering*

Udeda, S., Kimura, R., & Suzuki, K. (1975). Studies on the growth of the silkworm Bombyx mori. IV mutual relationship between the growth in the fifth instar larvae and productivity of silk substance and eggs. *Bulletin of the Sericultural Experiment Station*, *26*(3), 233–247.

Chapter - 5

Motivational Factors for Agripreneurship in Saitual Cluster

This chapter proposes to understand the motives that spurred the agripreneurs to start their agri-enterprises in Saitual.

1. Introduction

The word 'motivation' originates from the Latin word 'movere' which means to move. It is an inner urge in an individual that drives him/her towards a certain goal. Entrepreneurship involves human agency. The entrepreneurial process occurs because people are motivated to pursue and exploit perceived opportunities. It is rooted in the theory that action is the result of motivation and cognition (Diana et al, 2012). According to Herron and Sapienza (1992) motivation plays an important part in the creation of new organizations, theories of organization creation that fail to address this notion are incomplete. The concept of motivation is used to explain the direction, effort and persistency of action (Kanfer, 1990). Locke and Latham (1990) observed that motivation refers to factors within an individual, other than knowledge, which energize, direct and sustain behavior. According to Bird (1989), entrepreneurial motivation is manifested in the entrepreneur's vision and goals and it bears upon planning and behavior.

One way to explain entrepreneurial aspiration levels is by means of motives (Kolvereid 1992; Amit et al 2001; Morris et al 2006; Cassar 2007). People usually desire personal profits for autonomy amongst others or are just forced into entrepreneurship because they do not have any other option (Shane et al 2003; Locke and Baum 2007).

Several motivational theories have been propounded by psychologists to understand the urge that spurs entrepreneurs towards entrepreneurship. Research on entrepreneurship shed light on many motivational factors such as achievement motive (McClelland, 1961), power motive and self-discipline (McClelland 1961 and Burnham 1976), self-efficacy (Baum, 1994), locus of control (McClelland,1961 and Rotter, 1966), desire for autonomy (Burtner and Moore, 1997), independence (Hisrich, 1985, Hornaday and Aboud, 1973, and Aldridge, 1997), drive (Shane et al, 2003) and passion (Baum et al, 2001 and Shane et al, 2003). Literature has also elaborated on the environmental characteristics influencing the foundings of a firm (Aldrich, 2000) and the characteristics of entrepreneurial opportunities (Christiansen, 1997).

Ollenburg and Buckley (2007) in their study identified empirically, through a principal component analysis, five principal components: economic, family, social, independence, and retirement. Furthermore, McGehee and Kim (2004) made a distinction between the social and the economic factors as key motivations. Among factors of economic motivation, they included resource utilization, employment of family members, interest, and other factors. In addressing farmers diversifying into tourism in North Eastern England, Sharpley and Vass (2006) also addressed the motives of farmers and found that the need for extra income emerged as the most significant reason for diversification.

Literature suggests that an understanding of the motivational factors that surround entrepreneurial decision making is key in appreciating the dynamics of the entrepreneurial process and behavior (Kuratko et al. 1997; Robichaud et al. 2010). Several factors have been identified as the motivators for entrepreneurial engagement.

According to Gangadhara Rao (1986), the motivations of every individual are leveraged on his or her ambitions. He opined that ambition is the mother of all motives and it nourishes the achievement motivation. Shane et al (2003) observed that ambition influences the degree to which entrepreneurs seek to create something great, important and significant when they pursue opportunities and the nature of ambition may include making money or the desire to create something new from conception to actuality.

Gangadhara Rao (1986) futher observed that many a time it is the compulsion rather than the ambition that leads the man to success such as sudden unemployment that forces a change in occupation, opting for entrepreneurship as a last resort when all avenues to employment are closed and many others.

In order to have a full understanding of the role of motivation in the overall process of entrepreneurship in Saitual cluster, the present study has enquired into several entrepreneurial motivations that initiated the agripreneurs into sericulture industry. The study has also enquired whether they would like their children to continue as entrepreneurs in the same industry.

Motives can also be classified as either opportunity or necessity (Reynolds et al, 2001; Acs 2006), a distinction akin to "pull" and "push" (as cited in Hessels et al, 2008). Literature suggests that 'pull' motives such as autonomy (independence, freedom), income and wealth, challenge and recognition and status are reported in studies mostly conducted in developed countries (Kolvereid 1996; Feldman an Bolino 2000; Carter et al 2003). However, individuals may also be pushed into entrepreneurship (Thurik et al. 2008). Necessity motives occur for e.g when (a threat of) unemployment forces people into self-employment (Hessel et al. 2008). Studies suggest that necessity motives play a major role in developing countries, albeit to a lower extent in developed countries (Reynolds et al. 2002; Grilo and Thurik 2006; Bhola et al. 2006).Hessetls et al (2008), observed that these entrepreneurial motivations may determine the goals and aspirations for the firm, which in turn may determine macroeconomic outcomes. It is hence vital to understand the motivational factors that spur entrepreneurship in Saitual cluster.

Based on literature on entrepreneurial motives (Hessels et al 2008; Shane et al 2003; Locke and Baum 2007; Shane et al 1991; Thurik et al 2008; Reynolds et al 2001; ACS 2006; Khanka 2009) ten statements were put forth to the respondents to understand what factors motivated them to become agripreneurs. The entrepreneurs were asked to mark the appropriate slots on a five points scale ranging from 1-5 indicating strongly disagree to strongly agree, reflecting their views on the factors that motivated them.

2. Motivational Factors of Agripreneurs

The present study has identified several motivational factors that could have led to entrepreneurship in the cluster viz. 'to earn a livelihood', 'to get employment', 'to give financial security to my family (Necessity Motives) ; 'to gain independence', 'to gain social prestige', 'Enjoyment of the work' (Independent Motives); 'to earn money'; 'to make use of idle funds'; 'to diversify my economic interests', 'influenced by the success stories of other entrepreneurs' (Increase-wealth motives). Necessity motive indicates participation in entrepreneurial activity primarily because they have no other options for work whereas independence motive indicates the need for entrepreneurs to gain independence. Increasing wealth motive indicate that the prime motive for becoming an entrepreneurs as to increase wealth (Hessels et al 2008). The motivational factors that could have influenced the entrepreneurs are exhibited in Table 5.1.

Mean scores measured on a 5 point scale are used (Khanka 2009) to assess the motivational factors of small agripreneurs are farmers who own less than one acre of land, medium who own 1-2 acres of land and large agripreneurs are those who own more than 2 acres of land. Further in order to get a clear understanding of the motives that drive these agripreneurs, Kruskal Wallis (H Test) was used to identify various motives to small and medium and large farmers. The research has attempted to understand whether there is a variation in motives that drives entrepreneurial aspirations of these farmers on the basis of their land holdings. Accordingly, hypotheses were framed to test each motivational factor on the basis of land holding of the agripreneurs classified as small, medium and large. Wherever the hypothesis was rejected the researcher attempted to find out the relationship of that motive vis-à-vis small, medium and large farmers using H Test as a tool.

Table 5.1: **Factors that Influenced the Entrepreneur in Starting the Business**

Rank	*Factors*	*Mean Score*
1.	I started this business to earn money.	4.2
2.	I started this business to earn a livelihood.	4.1
3.	I started this business to give financial security to my family.	4.0
4.	I started this business because I enjoy the work.	3.89
5.	I started this business to gain independence	3.87
6.	I started this business to diversify my economic interests.	3.86
7.	I started this business as I was influenced by the success stories of other entrepreneurs.	3.12
8.	I started this business because I was unemployed	2.58
9.	I started this business to gain social prestige	2.5
10.	I started this business to make use of idle funds.	1.96

Source: Field Work.

1. To earn money

Although the ambition of livelihood and making money may seem similar, there is a sense inevitability in the choice of livelihood, whereas making money gives an impression of progression in the motivational theory propounded by Maslow (1954), that human needs follow a hierarchical order from lower to higher order needs, namely; physiological, security, social, self-esteem and self-actualization in that order (Ramswamy & Jyoti Kumar, 2012).

'Making money' emerged as the most significant motivational factor for the farmer entrepreneur (with a mean score of 4.2) in Saitual. Studies have shown that this factor has been as an important motivator for farmers.

The present study tested the hypothesis "There is no significant relationship between the size of the farm holding and the motive 'to earn money'" to find variation in the levels of motives among small, medium and large agripreneurs.

Table 5.2: To Earn Money

	Farmer's Size	*N*	*Mean Rank*
I started this business	Small	40	70.96
to earn money	Medium	86	95.05
	Large	54	97.73
	Total	180	

Table 5.3: Kruskal Wallis *H*-Test Statistics[a,b]

	I started this business to earn money
Chi-Square	10.846
df	2
Asymp. Sig.	.004

(a) Kruskal Wallis Test

(b) Grouping Variable: Size of farmer's land holding.

H_{o1}: There is no significant relationship between the size of the farm holding and the motive 'to earn money'

H_{11}: There is a significant relationship between the size of the farm holding and the motive 'to earn money'

Result:

Since the p value (0.004) < 0.05 (significance level) we reject the null hypothesis and conclude that there is a significant relationship between the size of the farm holding and the motive 'to earn money.' To examine the relationship further, analysis has been done on different group of farmers – 'small and medium farmers' and 'medium and large farmers'.

Table 5.4: Kruskal Wallis Test Statistics [a,b] –Small and Medium Farmers

	I started this business to earn money
Chi-Square	8.921
df Asymp. Sig.	1
	.003

(a) Kruskal Wallis Test

(b) Grouping Variable: Size of farmer's land holding.

H_{ola}: *There is no significant relationship between small and medium farmers and the motive 'to earn money'.*

H_{IIa}: *There is a significant relationship between small and medium farmers and the motive 'to earn money'*

Result:

Since the p value (0.003) < 0.05 (significance level) we will reject the null hypothesis and therefore conclude that there is significant relationship between small and medium farmers and the motive 'to earn money'

Interestingly the hypothesis was rejected. It is evident that the motive 'to earn money' has played a dominant role in the entrepreneurial aspirations of the large farmers. As mentioned earlier, 'pull' motives such as 'increasing income' are mostly prevalent in developed countries. It is evident that the large farmers are more driven by this motive as compared to the small and medium.

Table 5.5: Kruskal Wallis Test Statistics [a,b] –Medium and Large Farmers

	I started this business to earn money
Chi-Square	.110
df Asymp.	1
Sig.	.740

(a) Kruskal Wallis Test

(b) Grouping Variable: Size of farmer's land holding

H_{olb}: *There is no significant relationship between medium and large farmers and the motive 'to earn money'.*

H_{IIb}: *There is a significant relationship between medium and large farmers and the motive 'to earn money'*

Result: Since the p value (0.740) > 0.05 (significance level) we will fail to reject the null hypothesis and therefore conclude that there is no significant relationship between medium and large farmers and the motive 'to earn money'

These results imply that the motive "to earn money" has played a significant role in the entrepreneurial aspirations of medium farmers whereas it has not played a significant role in the entrepreneurial aspirations of small farmers.

Further, the researcher examined the relationship of the motive "to earn money" between 'medium and large' farmers. Notably, the results imply that it has played a significant role in the entrepreneurial aspirations of medium and large farmers.

However, for the small farmers, this "pull motive" has not played a significant role in their decision to take up entrepreneurship.

2. Earning a livelihood

Sometimes people are just forced into entrepreneurship because they have no other option (Shane et al. 2003; Locke and Baum 2007). This motivational factor (necessity entrepreneurship) is more common in lower income countries and decreases with the level of economic development (Wennekers et al. 2005).

Earning a livelihood emerged as the second most significant motivational factors for the farmer entrepreneur (with a mean of 4.1). Research evidence shows that 'making a living' has been a prime motivator for entrepreneurs (mainly women) in transitional economies (Bewayo 1995; Mishra 2000; Baruah 2000).

Livelihood generation is one of the major potentials of sericulture and silk industry. Perceptibly it is a source of sustainable livelihood for sericulture farmers in the cluster. This may be attributed to the fact that sericulture is an important cash crop with minimum investment, low gestation period, high employment potential and highly remunerative return. It is well suited to the agrarian economy of the tribals. Sericulture provides gainful employment to every section of society, a big farmer or a landless, aged person or a youth, man or a woman. It involves simple technology, which is easy to understand and adopt. Sericulture has provided downstream employment and income generation in rural and semiurban areas, high participation for low-income and socially under privileged groups. (Dewangan, 2017).

In India the labour intensive nature of sericulture industry is seen as strength and not weakness, as it provides employment to millions, especially in rural areas. Sericulture generates a higher income and employment per unit area and ensures a continuous and assured flow of income to the farmer throughout the year. The changes in employment and income opportunities in rural areas may be brought about by selecting a highly labour intensive and high income generating cropping system and sericulture has been identified as one such sector which plays a vital role in generating gainful employment opportunities to the villages (Ahsan, 2000).

Sericulture is providing stable income to many rural agricultural families and a livelihood to scores of landless farm and non-farm women labourers giving much economic strength. It is estimated that sericulture offers employment to around six million persons in India who are predominantly from the weaker sections of the society. The labour requirement in sericulture is more than four times that of paddy and five times that of ground nut (Rahmathulla and Geethadevi, 2000). It is also estimated that one hectare of land provides employment to approximately 10 persons throughout the year in various activities of sericulture industry and so sericulture can be considered as a model for self-employment and to uplift the economically poorer sections of the society in the developing countries like India (Ramakrishna Naika and Reddy, 1995).

Table 5.6: To Earn a livelihood

	Farmer's Size	*N*	*Mean Rank*
I started this business to		40	82.39
Small earn a livelihood	Medium	86	93.43
	Large	54	91.84
	Total	180	

Table 5.7: Kruskal Wallis Test Statistics[a,b]

	I started this business to earn money
Chi-Square	2.234
df	2
Asymp. Sig.	.327

(a) Kruskal Wallis Test

(b) Grouping Variable: Size of farmer's landholding

H_{o2}: There is no significant relationship between the size of the farm holding and the motive 'to earn a livelihood'

H_{12}: There is a significant relationship between the size of the farm holding and the motive 'to earn a livelihood'.

Result:

Since the p value is (0.327) > 0.05 (significance level), we will fail to reject the null hypothesis and therefore conclude that there is no significant relationship between the size of the farm holding and the motive 'to earn a livelihood.'

This motivational factor emerged as the second most important entrepreneurial motive of the agripreneurs in Saitual Cluster with the score of 4.1. Further, the hypothesis was rejected, which clearly shows that all the agripreneurs considered sericulture as a livelihood option irrespective of the land holding. This corroborates research evidence that necessity motives play a predominant role in the aspirations of entrepreneurs in developing countries.

Sericulture it plays a vital role in regulating seasonal unemployment. The amount of human labour per acre of sericulture is more than four times of sugarcane which is an annual crop. Even in the case of double cropping of paddy or groundnut human labour requirement per annum is less then sericulture. With four to five cycles of mulberry cultivation in a year, sericulture ensures employment throughout the year (Naidu E.M and Naidu B.J 1984). In his study, Chandrashekar Reddy T. (1987), he clearly pointed out that sericulture generates 411.15 man days whereas irrigated paddy produced 48.15 mandays compared to sugarcane of 240.28 man days. It is evident that sericulture has emerged as a sustainable livelihood option for the farmers of Saitual cluster.

3. Financial security to family

Financial security emerged as another significant motivating factor for farmers to enter the industry with a mean of 4.0. As mentioned earlier, sericulture plays an important role in providing financial security to a family as it assures regular employment and periodic returns round the year.

Hajare et al. (2008) observed that the contribution from sericulture enterprise was found to be highest at 52 percent (82315/ha/yr) followed by paddy-sunflower (20 %), soybeanwheat (15 %) and soybean-gram (12 %) in paddy area, whereas it was as high as 54 percent followed by cotton-pigeon pea (17 %), soybean-wheat (16 %) and soybean-gram (13 %) in cotton area and sustained income continued up to 15-20 years.

Srinivasa et al (2008) in their study conducted in Chamajanagar and Kolar districts of Karnataka during 2002-2003 revealed that the production cost of mulberry leaf was 6,528.00 acre / year in Chamarajanagar district and 31,929.00 / acre / year in Kolar district. The total cost of silkworm cocoon production was 16,520.00 and 77,780.00 / acre / year in the case of Chamarajanagar and Kolar districts respectively. The total return was 11,566.00 / acre / year and 1,25,954.00 / acre / year and the net return was

4,684.00 and 48,168.00 acre / year in the case of Chamarajanagar and Kolar districts respectively.

Yadaiah and Sarangapani (1994) in their study found that the costs and employment generation in sericulture enterprise in Warangal district of Andhra Pradesh was about 923.31 man days and the total cost was 13,902.57 per hectare. Sericulture was found to be the most beneficial enterprise in those drought-prone areas. Jagannathan (1995) studied the costs and returns structure and employment generation in sericulture enterprise in Coimbatore district of Tamil Nadu and observed that the cost declined with the increase in size of the farms (marginal, small, medium and big). The cost incurred ranged from 12,000.37 per hectare in the case of marginal farms to 10,763.62 per hectare in the case of big farmers. The net income between marginal farmers and big farmers ranged between 13,779.63 and 29,073.43. In this backdrop the hypothesis "There is no relationship between the size of the farm holding and the motive 'to give financial security to family'" was tested to understand whether there was any variation in the motive on the basis of land holding of the agripreneurs in Saitual.

Table 5.8: Financial Security to Family

	Farmer's Size	*N*	*Mean Rank*
I started this business to give financial security to my family.	Small	40	89.58
	Medium	86	92.16
	Large	54	88.54
	Total	180	

Table 5.9: Kruskal Wallis Test Statistics[a,b]

	I started this business to earn money
Chi-Square	.342
df Asymp. Sig.	2
	.843

(a) Kruskal Wallis Test

(b) Grouping Variable: Size of farmer's land holding

H_{03}: There is no significant relationship between the size of the farm holding and the motive 'to give financial security to family'.

H_{13}: There is a significant relationship between the size of the farm holding and the motive 'to give financial security to family'.

Result:

Since the p value is (0.843) > 0.05 (significance level), we will fail to reject the null hypothesis and therefore that there is no significant relationship between the size of the farm holding and the motive 'To give financial security to family'.

4. Enjoying the work

Enjoyable work falls within the purview of nature of work. It implies one's intrinsic interest in his/her work. For example, job enrichment may make the work enjoyable and interesting to the entrepreneurs. This factor is suggestive of the fact that achievers like to engage in those tasks they like and enjoy, and not just the task assigned to them (Khanka, 2009). Passion for work or love for one's own work has been identified in a qualitative analysis by Locke (2000) as a core characteristics of great wealth.

Researchers also claimed that passion for work is a characteristic of successful business leaders and passion is relevant in the entrepreneurship setting. (Bass and Stogdill 1990; House and Shamir 1993). Timmons (2000) also observed that passion is relevant in the entrepreneurship setting because it drives entrepreneurs to face extreme uncertainty and resource shortages.

This motive was accorded the fourth rank by the farmer entrepreneurs with a mean of 3.89. Sericulture is a labour intensive industry where labour is required in silk cocoon production for different operations such as cultivation of mulberry plants, harvesting of mulberry leaves, transporting of leaves from the garden to the rearing centre, feeding silk worms, cleaning beds placing the ripe silkworms on mountages and finally collecting the cocoons from mountages. Due to the requirement of labourer in each stage of silkwork rearing the bigger the size of the farms the more the participation of hired labourers, all of the large farmers in the cluster have employed hired labourers. However in a study conducted in Byadanur village observed that across the size classes the family labourers of landless, marginal and small farmers are fully involved in all the activities. Medium and large farmers have engaged hired labourers in Saitual. They have been engaged in the harvesting of leaves, exchanging of trays, cleaning of trays and other sericultural equipments mountages and harvesting of cocoons. Generally hired male labourers were engaged in harvesting of leaves because it needs hard labour to cut the stem of mulberry plant in the case of shoot harvest. It is clear that that it takes lots of hardwork for the farmers and their families involved to carry out the activities however it is evident that the farmers enjoy the work. In a similar study conducted by Rodi (2013) on farmers selling vegetables in Aizawl, she found that the farmers enjoyed their work.

It is evident that the agripreneurs enjoyed the work activities of sericulture.

Table 5.10: Enjoying the work

	Farmer's Size	*N*	*Mean Rank*
I started this business because I enjoy the work.	Small	40	81.33 93.97 91.78
	Medium	86	
	Large	54	
	Total	180	

Table 5.11: Kruskal Wallis Test Statistics[a,b]

	I started this business because I enjoy the work.
Chi-Square df	2.107
Asymp. Sig.	2
	.349

(a) Kruskal Wallis Test

(b) Grouping Variable: Size of farmer's land holding

H_{04}: There is no significant relationship between the size of the farm holding and the motive 'enjoyment of work'.

H_{14}: There is a significant relationship between the size of the farm holding and the motive 'enjoyment of work'.

Result:

Since the p value is (0.349) > 0.05 (significance level), we will fail to reject the null hypothesis and therefore conclude that there is no significant relationship between the size of the farm holding and the motive 'enjoyment of work'.

The hypothesis was failed to be rejected indicating that all the agripreneurs in Saitual irrespective of their land holdings enjoyed the work of sericulture.

5. To gain independence

Several researchers (Hisrich 1985; Hornaday and Aboud 1973; Aldridge 1997; Khanka 2009) have observed that 'gaining independence' has been a predominant motivational factor in the emergence of entrepreneurship. Entrepreneurship is likely to be a vehicle to serve the freedom-related needs of the individual as it enables a lifestyle in which one can decide oneself on goals, methods and time scheduling (Breaugh, 1999). Autonomy is valued by some for its own sake (Van Gelderen and Jansen 2006). Autonomy or independence is one of the most cited 'pull' factors for starting a business (Shane et al. 1991; Kolvereid 1996; Carter et al 2003; Van Gelderen and Jansen 2006). As mentioned earlier, pull motives are classified as opportunity factors which are more often reported in studies conducted on entrepreneurship in developed countries as opposed to push factors which play a major role in developed countries. It also involves taking responsibility of one's own life rather than living off the efforts of others. (Shane et al. 2003).

'Gaining independence' has not emerged as a significant motive for the agripreneurs with a mean score of only 3.87. Sericulture is a labour intensive rural industry, which does not require great skill but needs some care and delicacy in handling of silkworms. Thus, both skilled and unskilled, women, aged, and even children can undertake sericulture activity. Today many educated youth are coming forward to take up sericulture as agro-based rural industry under self-employment programme of the government.

5.12: To Gain Independence

	Farmer's Size	*N*	*Mean Rank*
I started this business to gain independenc	Small	40	83.50 88.47 98.93
	Medium	86	
	Large	54	
	Total	180	

Table 5.13: Kruskal Wallis Test Statistics[a,b]

	I started this business to gain independence
Chi-Square	3.072
df Asymp. Sig.	2
.	215

(a) Kruskal Wallis Test

(b) Grouping Variable: Size of farmer's land holding

H_{05}: There is no significant relationship between the size of the farm holding and the motive 'to gain independence'

H_{15}: There is a significant relationship between the size of the farm holding and the motive 'to gain independence'.

Result:

Since the p value is (0.215) > 0.05 (significance level), we will fail to reject the null hypothesis and therefore conclude that there is no significant relationship between the size of the farm holding and the motive 'to gain independence.'

Further, the hypothesis was tested and failed to be rejected which proves that this is not a dominant motive for the agripreneurs of Saitual cluster irrespective of the size of land holdings.

6. To diversify economic interest

Diversifying economic interest has been accorded a mean score of 3.86 by the agripreneurs. Interestingly, agripreneurs have not been driven by the motive of diversification of economic interests. This hypothesis was also rejected indicating no variation in this motivational aspiration among different types of farmers.

Table 5.14: To Diversify Economic Interest

	Farmer's Size	*N*	*Mean Rank*
I started this business to diversify my economic interests.	Small	40	89.65
	Medium	86	91.41
	Large	54	89.68
	Total	180	

Table 5.15: Kruskal Wallis Test Statistics[a,b]

	I started this business to diversify my economic interests.
Chi-Square	.102
df Asymp.	2
Sig.	.950

(a) Kruskal Wallis Test

(b) Grouping Variable: Size of farmer's land holding

H_{06}: There is no significant relationship between the size of the farm holding and the motive 'to diversify my economic interests'.

H_{16}: There is a significant relationship between the size of the farm holding and the motive 'to diversify my economic interests'.

Result:

Since the p value is (0.95) > 0.05 (significance level), we will fail to reject the null hypothesis and therefore conclude that there is no significant relationship between the size of the farm holding and the motive 'to diversify my economic interests'.

7. Influenced by the success stories of other entrepreneurs

This motive was accorded the sixth rank by the agripreneurs with a mean score of 3.12.

Schumpeter sees the introduction of innovations as the key process of economic change. Innovations do not just occur, but always have their basis in the pre-existing economic structure. The force that induces the system to drift is entrepreneurial innovation, asking for acts of entrepreneurship, i.e. heroic efforts of 'new men' to break the circular flow of existing activity. As an entrepreneur innovates rather than invents, he is a 'first mover', a position rendering him temporary monopoly power with associated huge monopoly profits. In turn, the profits the entrepreneur makes attract imitators. This tendency of economic actors to imitate successful entrepreneurs also explains the wave-like movements of innovative activity in 'competitive capitalism', Schumpeter argues. Since the appearance of a risk-loving entrepreneur creates a favourable climate for others who are less venturesome, an upswing in economic development occurs. But not forever: as the chances for making profits are eroded by imitation of the original innovation, an economic boom is followed by a downswing. In other words, innovations tend to appear and disappear in 'swarms' or 'clusters'.

Porter (1998) also observed that local rivalry is highly motivating. Peer pressure amplifies competitive pressure within a cluster, even among noncompeting or indirectly competing companies. Pride and the desire to look good in the local community spur executives to attempt to outdo one another. Clusters also often make it easier to measure and compare performances because local rivals share general circumstances—for example, labor costs and local market access—and they perform similar activities. Companies within clusters typically have intimate knowledge of their suppliers' costs. Managers are able to compare costs and employees' performance with other local companies. Additionally, financial institutions can accumulate knowledge about the cluster that can be used to monitor performance.

Table 5.16: Influenced by Success Stories

	Farmer's Size	*N*	*Mean Rank*
I started this business as I was influenced by the success stories of other entrepreneurs.	Small	40	102.19
	Medium	86	92.23
	Large	54	79.08
	Total	180	

Table 5.17: Kruskal Wallis Test Statistics[a,b]

	I started this business as I was influenced by the success stories of other entrepreneurs.
Chi-Square	5.241
df	2
Asymp. Sig.	.073

(a) Kruskal Wallis Test

(b) Grouping Variable: Size of farmer's land holding.

H_{07}: There is no significant relationship between the size of the farm holding and the motive 'influenced by success stories'.

H_{17}: There is a significant relationship between the size of the farm holding and the motive 'influenced by success stories'.

Result:

Since the p value is (0.73) > 0.05 (significance level), we will fail to reject the null hypothesis and therefore conclude that there is no significant relationship between the size of the farm holding and the motive 'influenced by success stories'.

Interestingly, the agripreneurs of Saitual were not influenced by the success stories of other entrepreneur and this hypothesis also fails to be rejected.

8. Unemployment

Unemployment forces people into entrepreneurship often in developing countries. (Hessels et al 2008). This type of necessity motive plays a major role in developing countries, albeit to a lower extent in developed countries (Reynolds et al. 2002; Grilo and Thurik 2006; Bhola et al. 2006).It is a necessity motive that indicates participation in entrepreneurial activity primarily because they have no other options for work.Sericulture is a labor intensive industry and occupies a pivotal position from the point of providing employment and additional income to weaker sections.India is the only country in the world to produce all the four known varieties of silk including Mulberry, Eri, Tasar and Muga. In 2013-2014 the employment in sericulture sector were 7.85 million persons and increased to 8.51 in 2016- 17. The total raw silk production was 26480 MT in 2013-14 which is recorded as 30265 MT in 2016-17. The sericulture industry has witnessed a quantum jump in raw silk productivity. The crucial aspect of sericulture lies in its capacity to generate more employment both onfarm and off-farm activities, especially in rural areas. It provides profitable occupation to small and marginal farmers. Sericulture provides an excellent and unique opportunity for socio-economic progress in the context of developing country like India, being a highly labour intensive industry. Sericulture is rightly known as "Industry of the poor". Notably, more than half of the labour force used in cultivation of mulberry and silkworm rearing was contributed by women labour. (Dewangan, 2017).

It appears that for the farmers in Saitual unemployment was not the primary factor that led them to participate in Sericulture since this motive was accorded only 2.58 mean score. It is evident that the agripreneurs were already in the occupation of agriculture and sericulture opened avenues for profitable farming. The farmers were more driven by other motivational factors such as 'making a livelihood' and 'earning money'.

Table 5.18: Unemployment

	Farmer's Size	*N*	*Mean Rank*
I started this business because I was unemployed	Small	40	102.66
	Medium	86	83.83
	Large	54	92.11
	Total	180	

5.19: Kruskal Wallis Test Statistics[a,b]

	I started this business because I was unemployed
Chi Square 4.297 df 2 Asymp. Sig. 117	

(a) Kruskal Wallis Test

(b) Grouping Variable: Size of farmer's land holding

H_{08}: There is no significant relationship between the size of the farm holding and the motive 'to gain employment'.

H_{18}: There is a significant relationship between the size of the farm holding and the motive 'to gain employment'.

Result:

Since the p value is (0.117) > 0.05 (significance level), we fail to reject the null hypothesis and therefore conclude that there is no significant relationship between the size of the farm holding and the motive 'To gain employment'

The testing of the hypothesis also reveals that there was no variation in the motive among small, medium and large farmers.

9. To gain social prestige

Gaining social prestige is not a significant motive for the farmers having accorded a mean score of only 2.5. Pull motives include motives such as autonomy, independence, freedom, income and wealth, challenge and recognition and status (Kolvereid 1996; Fieldman and Bolino 2000; Cater et al. 2003; Wilson et al. 2004). Gaining social prestige indicates a movement of human needs of higher order needs in the pyramid Khanka (2009) referred 'Recognition and reputation' as a status motive and related it to Maslows ego or esteem needs in his study on Assamese entrepreneurs. This motive has played an insignificant role in the motivational aspirations of the agripreneurs in Saitual.

Table 5.20: To Gain Social Prestige

	Farmer's Size	*N*	*Mean Rank*
I started this business to gain social prestige	Small	40	93.25
	Medium	86	89.02
	Large	54	90.82
	Total	180	

Table 5.21: Kruskal Wallis Test Statistics[a,b]

	I started this business to gain social prestige
Chi-Square	.203
df Asymp.	2
Sig.	.904

(a) Kruskal Wallis Test

(b) Grouping Variable: Size of farmer's land holding

H_{09}: There is no significant relationship between the size of the farm holding and the motive 'to gain social prestige'

H_{19}: There is a significant relationship between the size of the farm holding and the motive 'to gain social prestige'.

Result:

Since the p value is (0.904) > 0.05 (significance level), we fail to reject the null hypothesis and therefore conclude that there is no significant relationship between the size of the farm holding and the motive 'to gain social prestige'.

Further, the hypothesis fails to be rejected, which indicates that this motive is insignificant in the emergence of entrepreneurship in Saitual cluster.

10. Make use of idle funds

Making use of idle funds is not a significant motive for the farmers having accorded the least mean score of 1.96.

Table 5.22: Make Use of Idle Funds

	Farmer's Size	*N*	*Mean Rank*
I started this business to make use of idle funds	Small	40	90.31
	Medium	86	90.46
	Large	54	90.70
	Total	180	

Table 5.23: Kruskal Wallis Test Statistics[a,b]

	I started this business to make use of idle funds
Chi-Square	.002
df Asymp.	2
Sig.	.999

(a) Kruskal Wallis Test

(b) Grouping Variable: Size of farmer's land holding.

H_{010}: There is no significant relationship between the size of the farm holding and the motive 'to make use of idle funds'.

H_{110}: There is a significant relationship between the size of the farm holding and the motive 'to make use of idle funds'.

Result:

Since the p value is (0.999) > 0.05 (significance level), we will fail to reject the null hypothesis and therefore conclude that there is no significant relationship between the size of the farm holding and the motive 'To make use of idle funds'

3. Promise of Entrepreneurship for the Next Generation

The study enquired into what aspiration sericulture holds for the entrepreneurs for their next generation. To this end the entrepreneurs were asked whether they would like their children to become entrepreneurs in the sericulture industry. It seems that from the point of view of majority of the farmers, sericulture holds promise for their children. 65 percent of the entrepreneurs would like their children to become entrepreneurs in the same business whereas about 35 percent of the entrepreneurs (63 in number) do not want their children to become entrepreneurs in sericulture industry.

The present study further elicited answers from 63 entrepreneurs about the reasons behind their not wanting their children to take up entrepreneurship in sericulture. A high majority of the farmers (71.43 percent) feel that their children may not be interested in taking up sericulture as a source of income and 19 percent of the farmers claim that sericulture is not profitable enough for their children to take up.

Table 5.24: Reasons for Children not Becoming Entrepreneurs

Reasons	*Frequency*	*Percentage*
No interest	45	71.43
It is not profitable	12	19.00
There is no future	2	3.17
Any other reason	4	6.35
Total	**63**	**100**

Source: Field Work.

Notably only 19% of the 63 entrepreneurs who feel that children would not be interested in this business perceived non profitability as an entry barrier for the next generation. It is evident that entrepreneurs perceive this business to be profitable. Further, only two farmers perceived 'no future' for their business.

Table 5.25: Willingness to adapt new ideas for your business

		Frequency	*Percent*	*Valid Percent*	*Cumulative Percent*
Valid	Yes	146	81.1	81.1	81.1
	No	3	1.7	1.7	82.8
	Don't know	30	16.7	16.7	99.4
	4.00	1	.6	.6	100.0
	Total	**180**	**100.0**	**100.0**	

An overwhelming majority of farmer entrepreneurs are willing to adopt new ideas for the growth of their business. It is evident new knowledge and skills imparted through training of these entrepreneurs will enhance their capabilities.

4. Conclusion

It is clear that "necessity motives" ('to earn a livelihood', 'to give financial security to my family) have played a predominant role in the agripreneurs opting for entrepreneurship in Saitual cluster. Whereas, the "independent motive" ('to gain independence') have not played a highly significant role in the emergence of entrepreneurship in Saitual cluster. In fact, the independent motive 'to gain social prestige' has emerged as one of the most insignificant motives. Interestingly, "increasing wealth" has been an important driver of entrepreneurial aspirations for large and medium farmers in the cluster. However, it was not a significant motive to small farmers.

Since necessity-motivated entrepreneurs are likely to depend heavily on their farm for daily economic survival, this may positively affect the aspirations they have for their firm (Hessels et at. 2008). Their aspirations will have an impact on the larger goals of development of the region. The analysis in the present study is in tandem with the observations of Wennekers et al. (2005), that necessity entrepreneurship is more common in lower income countries and decreases with the level of economic development.

References

Acs, Z.J. (2006). How is entrepreneurship good for economic growth?. Innovations, 1(1), 97–107.

Ahsan, M.M. (2000). Sericulture Status and Technologies for Cold and Temperate Conditions in India, Natl. Conf. Strat. Seric. Res. Dev. (Souvenir), 16-18 November 2000, CSR&TI, Mysore, 41-45.

Aldrich H (2000): Organizations evolving. Beverly Hills, Sage.

Aldridge, J.H. (1997). An Occupational Personality Profile of the Male entrepreneur as Assessed by the 16PF fifth edition, Unpublished doctoral dissertation, University of Georgia.

Amit, R., MacCrimmon, K.R., Zietsma, C., & Oesch, J.M. (2001). Does money matter: Wealth attainment as the motive for initiating growth-oriented technology ventures. *Journal of Business Venturing*, 16(2), 119–143.

Bass, B.M., & Stogdill, R.M. (1990). Bass & Stogdill's handbook of leadership: Theory, research, and managerial implications, New York: Free Press.

Baruah, S.S. (2000). Women Entrepreneurs in North East- Role of Training in Creating and Sustaining Micro enterprises', in Prabath, S, V, V Patil, C Rani, R Shukla and Rao Gopala (eds), *Women Entrepreneurs in India: Challenges and Achievements*, NISIET, Indian Express Newspapers Ltd, Hyderabad.

Baum, R. (1994). The Relation of Traits, Competencies, Vision, Motivation and Strategy to Venture Growth', unpublished doctoral dissertation, University of Maryland, College Park, MD.

Bewayo. & Edward, D. (1995). Uganda Entrepreneurs: Why they are in Business?, *Journal of Business Strategy*, 6(1), 67-78.

Bhola, R., Verheul, I., Grilo, I., & Thurik, A.R. (2006). Explaining engagement levels of opportunity and necessity entrepreneurs, Research report H200610. Zoetermeer: EIM Business and Policy Research.

Bird, B. (1988). Implementing entrepreneurial ideas: The case for intention. Academy of Management Review, 13(3), 442–453.

Breaugh, J.A. (1999). Further investigation of the work autonomy scales: Two studies.*Journal of Business and Psychology*, 13(3), 357–373.

Burtner E Holly, and DP Moore (1997): Women's Organizational Exodus to Entrepreneurship: Self-reported Motivations and Correlates with Success, *Journal of Small Business Management*, 35, 1, 34-46.

Carter, N.M., Gartner, W.B., Shaver, K.G., & Gatewood, E.J. (2003). The career reasons of nascent entrepreneurs. *Journal of Business Venturing*, 18(1), 13–39.

Cassar, G. (2007). Money, money, money? A longitudinal investigation of entrepreneur career reasons, growth preferences and achieved growth. *Entrepreneurship and Regional Development*, 19(1), 89–107.

Chandrashekar, R.T. (1987) Income and Employment generation in Sericulture via-vis alternative crops in Hosur Taluk in Dharmapuri District Univertsity ofAgricultural Sciences, Bangalore 1987

Christiansen, C. (1997). *The Innovators Dilemma*, Harvard Business School Press.

Dewangan, S.K. (2017). Sericulture play key role to employment generation and socio- economic empowerment of tribal women", *International Journal of Advanced Research and Development*, 2(6), 761-768.

Diana, M.H., Maija, R., & Charles, H.M. (2012). The nascent entrepreneurship hub: goals, entrepreneurial self-efficacy and start-up outcomes.

Feldman, D.C., & Bolino, M.C. (2000). Career patterns of the self-employed: Career motivations and career outcomes. *Journal of Small Business Management*, 38(1), 53–67.

Gangadhara, R.N. (1986). *Entrepreneurship and Growth of Enterprises in Industrial Estates*, Deep and Deep Publications Pvt. Ltd, New Delhi.

Government of Mizoram. (2012). Sericulture at a Glance, Information and Publicity Cell, Directorate of Sericulture, Aizawl, Mizoram.

Grilo, I., & Thurik A R (2006), "Entrepreneurship in the old and new Europe. In E. Santarelli (Ed.), Entrepreneurship, growth, and innovation: The dynamics of firms and industries: International studies in entrepreneurship", Berlin: Springer Science, pp. 75–103.

Hazare, T. N. & Jadav. (2008). Sericulture Brings Better Income. *Indian Silk,* 46 (9)

Hessels, J., Van, G.M., & Thurik, R. (2008). Drivers of entrepreneurial aspirations at the country level: the role of start-up motivations and social security. *International Entrepreneurship and Management Journal, forthcoming.*

Hisrich, R.D. (1985). The Woman Entrepreneur in the United States and Puerto Rico: a Comparative Study. *Leadership and Organizational Development Journal*, Vol. 5, 3–8.

Hornaday, J., & Aboud, J. (1973). Characteristics of Successful Entrepreneurs. *Personnel Psychology,* 24, 141–153.

House, R.J., & Shamir, B. (1993). Toward the integration of transformational, charismatic and visionary theories of leadership, In M. Chemers & R. Ayman (Eds.). *Leadership theory and research: Perspectives and directions*, San Diego, CA: Academic Press, 81–107.

Jagannathan, N. (1995). Impacts of sericulture on income and employment generation. *Indian Silk*, 33, 11-16.

Khanka, S.S. (2009). Motivational Orientation of Assamese Entrepreneurs in the SME Sector. *The Journal of Entrepreneurship*, 18(2), 209–218.

Kolvereid, L. (1992). Growth aspirations among Norwegian entrepreneurs. *Journal of Business Venturing*, 7(3), 209–222.

Kolvereid, L. (1996). Organizational employment versus self-employment: Reasons for career choice intentions. *Entrepreneurship Theory and Practice*, 20(3), 23–31.

Locke, E.A., & Latham, G. (1990). A theory of goal setting and task performance, Englewood Cliffs, New Jersey: Prentice Hall.

Locke, E.A. (2000). *The prime movers.* New York: Amacom.

Locke, E.A., & Baum, J.R. (2007). Entrepreneurial motivation. In J. R. Baum, M. Frese, & R. A. Baron (Eds.), The psychology of entrepreneurship, Mahwah, NJ: Erlbaum, 93–112.

Maslow, A.H. (1954). Motivation and Personality, New York: Harper & Row.

McClelland, D.C. (1961). The achieving society, Princeton:Van Nostrand.

McClelland, D.C., & David, H.B. (1976). *Power is the Great Motivator*, Harvard Business Review Classics, HBR.

Mishra, P. (2000). Women Entrepreneurs: are They Enterprising and Empowered Enough? - A Study in Small Scale Industrial sector of Orissa, in Prabath, S, V, V Patil, C Rani, R Shukla and Rao Gopala, (eds), *Women Entrepreneurs in India: Challenges and Achievements*, NISIET, Indian Express Newspapers Ltd, Hyderabad, pp 142-154.

Morris, M.H., Miyasaki, N.N., Watters, C.E., & Coombes, S.M. (2006). The dilemma of growth: Understanding venture size choices of women entrepreneurs. *Journal of Small Business Management,* 44(2), 221–244.

Naidu, E.M., & Naidu, B.J. (1984) Sericulture and Rural development in 7th plan, Southern Economist 1984, 23 (2), 23-25.

Ollenburg, C., & Buckley, R. (2007). Stated Economic and Social Motivations of Farm Tourism Operators. *Journal of Travel Research*, SAGE Publications, 45(4), 445447.

Ostwald, M., Jonsson, A., Wibeck, V., & Asplund, T. (2012). Mapping energy crop cultivation and identifying motivational factors among Swedish farmers, *Biomass & Bioenergy,* 50, 25-34.

Porter, M. (1998). On Competition: New Agendas for Companies, Governments and Institutions, Harvard Business School Press, Boston.

Rahmathulla, V.K., & Geethadevi, R.G. (2000). Sericulture – An apt venture for rural betterment, *Agriculture Today*, 3(4), 46-48.

Ramakrishna, N., & Reddy, D.N.R. (1995). Sericulture – A Role Model for Self employment. Farmer & Parliament, September: 19-20

Ramswamy, R., & Kumar J.N.V.R. (2012). Motivational Factors of Tribal Entrepreneurs in Handloom Clusters: A Case Study of Thenzawl, Mizoram. *IUP Journal of Entrepreneurship Development*, 9(4), 56-68.

Reynolds, P.D., Camp, S.M., Bygrave, W.D., Autio, E., & Hay, M. (2001). Global Entrepreneurship Monitor: 2001 Executive Report, Kansas City, MO: Kauffman Center for Entrepreneurial Leadership.

Reynolds, P.D., Bygrave, W.D., Autio E, Cox, L., & Hay, M. (2002). Global Entrepreneurship Monitor: 2002 Executive Report", Kansas City, MO: Kauffman Center for Entrepreneurial Leadership.

Rodi, L. (2013). Unpublished MPhil Thesis "Entrepreneurship among street vendors of vegetables in Aizawl, Mizoram, (MPhil Thesis, Department of Commerce, Mizoram University).

Rotter, J.B. (1966). Generalized expectancies for internal versus external control of reinforcement. Psychological Monographs: General and Applied, 80, 609.

Shane, S., Kolvereid, L., & Westhead, P. (1991). An exploratory examination of the reasons leading to new firm formation across country and gender. *Journal of Business Venturing*, 6(6), 431–446.

Shane, S., Locke, E.A., & Collins, C.J. (2003). Entrepreneurial motivation. Human Resource Management, Review 13, 257–279.

Srinivasa, G., Kumaresan, P., & Vijayaprakash, N.B. (2008). Economic analysis of resource use efficiency in sericulture. *Indian Journal of Sericulture*. 47(1), 29-33.

Thurik, A.R., Carreer, M.A., Van, S.A.J., & Audretsch, D.B. (2008). Does self-employment reduce unemployment?, *Journal of Business Venturing, forthcoming*.

Timmons, J.A. (2000). New venture creation: Entrepreneurship (5th ed.). Homewood, IL: Irwin. Van, G.M.W., & Jansen, P.G.W. (2006). Autonomy as a startup motive. *Journal of Small Business and Enterprise Development*, 13(1), 23–32.

Wennekers, S., Van, S.A., Thurik, R., & Reynolds, P. (2005). Nascent entrepreneurship and the level of economic development. *Small Business Economics*, 24(3), 293–309.

Wilson, F., Marlino, D., & Kickul, J. (2004). Our entrepreneurial future: Examining the diverse attitudes and motivations of teens across gender and ethnic identity. *Journal of Developmental Entrepreneurship*, 9(3), 177–197.

Yadaiah & Sarangapani. (1994). Economics of sericulture – A micro level study, Agri banker,17(1), 38-40.

Chapter - 6

Financial Performance of Sericulture Enterprises

1. Introduction

In this chapter, the researcher has attempted to estimate the financial performance of the agri enterpprises in Saitual cluster. Sericulture is a highly profitable activity and its profitability depends on the production of quality mulberry leaves and its conversion into quality cocoons at economic costs. Sericulture plays a vital role in rural development, as it integrates well with the farming systems and has the potential to generate attractive income throughout the year. It needs low capital and provides year round employment (Hanumappa and Erappa, 1985).

In view of this, it is imperative to understand the economics of sericulture and estimate the returns that accrue to the sericulturists in Saitual.

Table 6.1: Categorisation of sample farmers according to their mulberry land holdings.

Land holding of Agripreneurs	*No. of farmers*	*Percent*
Upto 1 acre	40	22.22
1 to 2 acres	86	47.8
Above 2 acres	54	30
Total	**180**	**100**

Source: Field Work.

At the outset a glimpse into the classification of farm holdings shows that the size for mulberry land holdings in the study area varies from 0.5 acres to 3 acres. The farm holdings are classified into three categories viz., less than one acre, one to two acres and more than two acres for analyzing the variables that influences sericulture activity. As indicated in the table 6.1, majority of land holdings are between one and two acres in the cluster.

It is clear from Table 6.1 that 22.22 percent of the farmers practicing sericulture owned less than one acre or land and 47.8 percent farmers were in the category one to two acres and around 30 percent farmers in the category of above two acres. The researcher has estimated the cost incurred and the returns for one acre in the present study.

As mentioned earlier, sericulture as an economic activity comprises of two main activities:

I. **MULBERRY CULTIVATION**– which includes *establishment of mulberry garden* (initial stage) and *recurring expenditure from second year onwards;*

II. **SILKWORM REARING** – which includes *quantity of silkworms reared per household* and *the expenditure involved in rearing;*

I. Mulberry Cultivation

1. Establishment of Mulberry Garden: (Initial Stage)

Mulberry is a perennial crop and the establishment of mulberry garden is a crucial factor in the success of the sericulture enterprise and hence the initial establishment cost is vital. Profitability from the enterprise largely depends on the quantity of mulberry leaves produced and which will impact the production of cocoons. As mentioned earlier, the average size of mulberry land holdings in Saitual was two acres. The researcher has adopted one acre as the economic unit for cocoon production for the analysis of the profitability of the enterprise. The data relating to the establishment cost was collected from the farmers during the field visit and has been presented in Table 6.2. The table presents estimated cost for establishment of once acre of mulberry farm. The researcher has estimated the expenditure incurred for cultivation of mulberry leaves in detail under the heads:

(a) Land Development

(b) Raising of Plantation

(c) Rearing Infrastructure

(d) Miscelleneous

Table 4 shows the various costs involved in establishment and management of one acre of mulberry garden in Saitual. The total estimated cost of establishment and management of one acre was Rs.1, 77,260. However, as the farmers have received subsidies in the form of rearing

Rs. 77,760 and Rs.50,000 under NLUP scheme from the Government of Mizoram, the actual cost incurred was only Rs.49,500 for one acre.

Table 6.2: Estimated cost of Initial establishment and management of one acre mulberry farm

Sl. No.	*Particulars*	*Qty. of Mandays*	*Rate per manday (Rs.)*	*Total Amount (Rs.)*
(a)	Land Development Clearing of jungle, burning, land preparation, etc. (Wages for mandays)	50	350	17,500
	Sub-Total			17,500
(b)	Raising of Plantation			
(i)	Cost of plantation			
	(a) Pit digging and spacing	50	350	24,500
	(b) Planting of sapling/cutting	40	350	14,000
	(c) Cost of manure	-	-	-
	(d) Weeding (4 times a year)	90	350	31,500
	Sub-Total			70,000
(c)	Rearing Infrastructure			
(i)	Construction of Rearing	1	40,000	40,000
(ii)	House - Assam type 24'×15' (Subsidy given by Government)			
	Rearing appliances			
	(a) Sintex*	1	5000	5000
	(b) Plastic Trays (2x3 feet)	50	350	17,500
	(c) Mountages (3x2 feet)	80	60	4,800
	(d) Rearing stands	15	300	4,500
	(e) Bed cleaning nets	80	50	4000
	(f) Disinfectant	5	150	750
	(g) Sprayers	3	190	570
	(h) Other appliances (Hydrometer, Chopping board, Towel etc)	1 each		590
	Sub-Total			77,760
(d)	Miscellaneous		12000	12000
	Total expenditure incurred:			**1,77,260**
(e)	Subsidies received:			
	(i) Rearing infrastructure and appliances		77,760	
	(ii) NLUP		50,000	**1,27,760**
	Total expenditure incurred by farmers = a+b+c+d-e			**49,500**

Source: Field Work

(a) *Land development:–* The farmers in Mizoram follow jhumming cultivation for land development which mainly involves clearing of jungle and burning for land preparation. It is evident from the table that a total mandays of around 50 days at a rate of Rs. 350 per manday was utilized in the initial year for carrying out land development activities and the total cost was estimated to be Rs.17, 500.

(b) *Raising of Plantation:—* Land development is followed by raising of plantation which involves activities such as cutting, pit digging, planting of sapling and weeding. Generally, pit system of planting with wider spacing is usually adopted for rainfed mulberry while row system with closer spacing is adopted for irrigated mulberry (Krishnaswami, 1986). As the mulberry plantation in Saitual are rainfed, pits were dug by the farmers These pits were filled with soil, preferably mixed with some cattle manure in which the cuttings or rooted saplings were planted. Pit digging and Planting of sapling required an estimated 50 and 40 mandays in a year at a rate of Rs.350 per manday respectively. Notably, the cost of manure is 'nil' in Table 6.2, which may be attributed to the fact that the soil of Mizoram is naturally suitable to grow a healthy mulberry garden without the help of fertilizers and farm yard manure. It was found during the field study that none of the farmers applied fertilizers to the farm.

Making the field weed free especially during the initial stage for good growth and yield of plant is critical. Weeding was done four times in a year at an interval of two to three months with a total mandays of 90 at the rate of Rs.350 per manday. The total cost of Raising of Plantation which included pit digging, planting of sapling/cutting and weeding was estimated at Rs. 70,000 in the first year of establishment of mulberry farm of one acre in Saitual cluster.

As mentioned in Table 6.2 subsidies given to the sericulturists in Saitual by the government of Mizoram as part of cluster development initiatives. (i) Rearing infrastructure which included - Construction of rearing house and Rearing and water storage equipments .The rearing of the mulberry silkworms was fully domesticated in Saitual. A silkworm-rearing house is the place where the silkworms are reared to produce cocoons. The cocoon quality and yield are adversely affected if the optimal environmental conditions i.e. temperature, relative humidity, ventilation, illumination, hygiene, etc. are not maintained. The rearing house should be rationally designed in order to keep the micro-climatic and environmental conditions for rapid and healthy growth of the silkworms. It should, therefore, have facilities for creation and maintenance of the optimal environmental conditions inside the silkworm-rearing house. The rearing house should also provide sufficient space and healthy environment for the workers attending the silkworm rearing (Central Silk Board). Interestingly, in Saitual cluster each of the farmers have availed Rs.40, 000 on average from the government to construct a rearing house (Assam type) 24'x15'as subsidy (Table 6.2).

Figure 3: Rearing House

Location: Saitual

The rearing house is usually equipped with different rearing equipment viz; Chandrika Mountages[1], Rearing Stands[2], plastic trays, Bed cleaning nets[3], sprayer, Disinfectant towels, as hydrometer and nets towel, knives and leaves chopping board and one Sintex (500 L) tank.

The details of the various equipments used for rearing silkworm in Saitual cluster are mentioned below (Table 6.2).

(a) Sintex tanks – As mentioned earlier, Saitual sericulture cluster rainfed and the sericulture department provided one Sintex (500 L) to each farmers for rain harvesting which was valued as

Rs.5000. The researcher observed that the farmers possessed one sintex tanks for storage of water during the field visit.

(b) Plastic trays – Initially, the female silk moth lays hundreds of eggs. These eggs are stored over a clean paper or piece of cloth. These eggs are then sold to the silkworm farmers. The farmers then kept the eggs under the accurate temperature and humidity at a clean place. They are kept warm in the most appropriate temperature to hatch eggs to produce larvae or caterpillar. This process is done when the mulberry trees have fresh crop of leaves. The caterpillar eats this mulberry leaves day and night and it grows in size.

Plastic trays are used to keep these caterpillars and some freshly chopped mulberry leaves are kept in the tray. After 30-40 days approximately the caterpillars stop eating the leaves and then it moves inside the small chambers in the bamboo trays to spin cocoons.

Figure 4: Plastic trays

These are produced by the secretion of liquid protein from their salivary glands. Small racks are given in the trays so that the cocoons get attached to those racks. Silk moths are developed inside the cocoons. In Saitual cluster, around 50 plastic trays (2×3 feet) were supplied to the farmers by the government for silkworm rearing for an average of one acre land holding.

(c) Mountages- The most important device that helps or supports the silkworms (larvae) for comfortable spinning their cocoon is called cocoonage or mountage. It determines both the quality and quantity of the cocoons. Different types of cocoonages are used in different parts of India. In general, these are made of wood, bamboo, cardbaord, plastic, grass, dry leaves, twigs, etc. In Saitual cluster the following types of mountages were used:-

(i) *Chandrikas:* This round- or rectangular- shaped mountage is made of bamboo mat supported by split bamboo reapers on all sides. On the mat, a bamboo tape of 4-5 cm width is wound in a spiral manner. About 1000 worms can be mounted on this mountage. These are easy to handle, repairable and cocoons spinned on Chandrika are of good quality.

(ii) *Plastic Mountage:* Like Chandrika, but is made from plastic instead of bamboo and hence, more durable, easy to clean, not prone to rodent attack, and produces lesser number of double cocoons. Once invested, further maintenance, care or expenditure are not incurred.

Figure 5: Plastic Mountage

(d) Rearing Stands– Silkworms are reared in bamboo or plastic trays which are arranged one over the other in tiers on rearing stands. Rearing stands were arranged in two rows parallel to the wall with adequate space in the centre, for removing the trays and for conducting the cleaning and feeding operations. Mulberry leaves were picked from the plants were cut to convenient size and fed to the silkworms. Usually 4 feeding were given in a day and nets were used for cleaning the beds. As shown in Table 6.2, around Rs.4,500 was given as a subsidy by the government for procurement of rearing stands for an average landholding of one acre.

(e) Bed cleaning nets– Young age silkworms are delicate and prone to diseases. Thus, maintenance of cleanliness in silkworm bed is a vital aspect to ensure hygiene in the rearing microclimate as well as for silkworm body. Time to time bed cleaning is essential to remove unused mulberry leaves and silkworm litters accumulated in the rearing bed. Cleaning is done by nylon net of mesh size one cm. sq. (1.00 cm2). Cleaning net is spread covering the full rearing bed just one feed before the cleaning time and the feeding was given above the net. At the time of next feed the net along with the larvae were transferred to another tray and fresh feed was given only after giving sufficient spacing (Central Silk Board, 2015). The farmers in Saitual utilised around 80 of these bed cleaning nets which normally cost around Rs. 50 each.

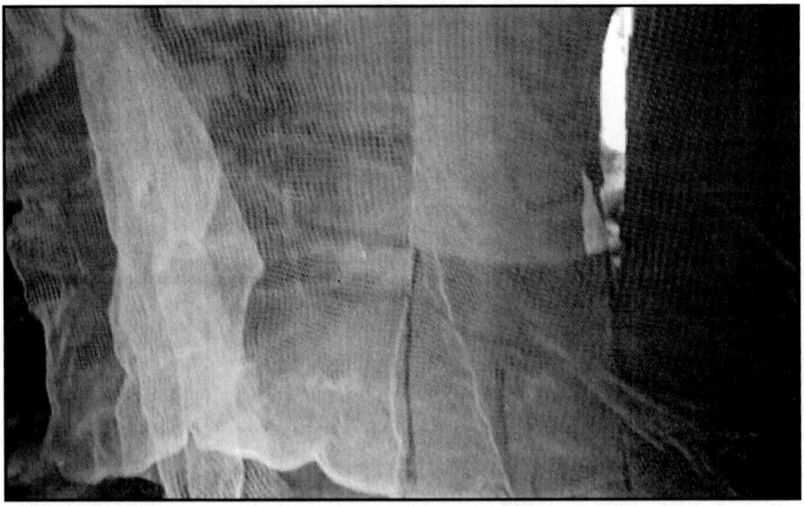

Figure 6: Nets

(f) Disinfectant– One of the major reasons for crop losses in cocoon production is the diseases of silkworms. Proper disinfection of rearing house, its surroundings and appliances and maintenance of hygiene are important to prevent diseases. Diseased silkworms extrude pathogens into the rearing environment that become the source of infection. Destruction of disease causing pathogens is called disinfection. Although it can be done by various methods, the most effective one is chemical method using chemical disinfectants For silkworm rearing the common disinfectants used are - Bleaching powder, Slaked lime, Chlorine dioxide (Sanitech) etc. (Central Silk Board, 2015). The farmers in Saitual used a chemical disinfectant called 'Ashtra Solution'. 50 g of Ashtra powder is dissolved in 100 litre of water and after keeping the solution of 2 hours it was sprayed using sprayer.

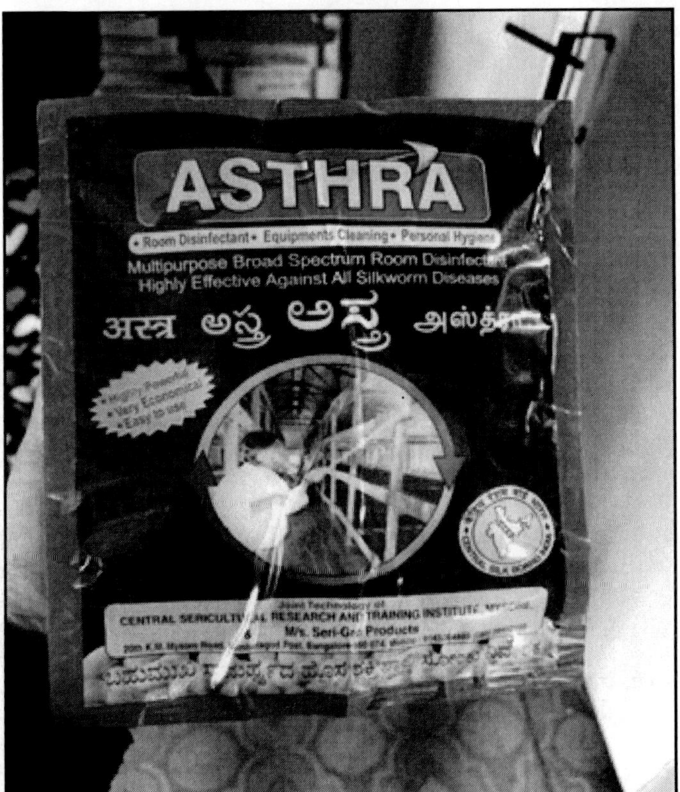

Figure 7: Disinfectant (Asthra)

(g) Sprayer– The rearing houses must be thoroughly disinfected for good cocoon crop. Power sprayers are very effective and fast for disinfection of rearing houses and rearing equipments. Electricity and engine operated sprayers have gained popularity among farmers due to effectiveness and fastness in carrying out disinfection (CSRTI, 2008). In Saitual cluster sprayers were used for disinfection of rearing houses, rearing stands and mountages.

(h) Other appliances– Other appliances such as hydrometer, towel, knives and leaves chopping board are some of the important items used for rearing of silkworms by the farmers. These equipment were also supplied by the government to the farmers as subsidy.

As shown in Table 6.2, the total cost on construction of rearing house and for rearing equipment was estimated at Rs.77, 760 which was entirely subsidized by the

Government of Mizoram ii) NLUP - It is pertinent to note that each of the farmers of the cluster received Rs.50, 000 on average from the government under the NLUP scheme. As mentioned earlier Saitual is an "induced cluster" where entrepreneurship has emerged as an outcome of cluster development activities initiated by Government of Mizoram through NLUP and Cluster Area Development Project (CADP).

The main aim of the NLUP was to develop suitable and stable trades for the farmers in the state. The Policy also aimed at providing the village farmers selfsufficiency in rice, vegetables etc. and subsidies to enable them to take up occupation on farm based work. The numbers of farmers covered under NLUP were 2096 in 2011-12 in Mizoram and it has been observed that an overwhelming number of farmers in Saitual sericulture cluster were also selected under the scheme of NLUP.

Saitual cluster started to take its form in 1994 with one farmer engaging in sericulture for commercial purposes. The period between 2009-14 witnessed the birth of majority of the units (76 percent). This period coincided with the launching of the 'Cluster Area Development Project' (CDP) which included Saitual cluster as on 2011-2012.

Hence, the farmers of the cluster also received Rs.50,000 under the New Land Use (NLUP)scheme to start up their sericulture units.

Hence, the estimated cost actually incurred by the farmers the initial year was Rs. 49500 (70 percent of the total estimated cost of Rs.1, 77,260). The mulberry garden once established is expected to give yield for 12 to 15 years. It was observed that during the first year the number of crops harvested was not optimum and the productivity of the crop is also low. Over the years, however, the sericulturists in Saitual have gained knowledge and experience and improved their performance and productivity levels.

The researcher has further estimated the Recurring expenditure on one acre of established mulberry garden from the second year onwards (Table 6.3)

2. Recurring Expenditure from second year onwards

The sericulture farmer incurs a significant expenditure in the first year of establishing expenditure. Thereafter, the agripreneur incurs only the recurring expenditure which have been examined in Table 6.3. The expenses incurred are listed in Table 6.3.

Recurring expenditure on rearing broadly includes (a) Cultivation expenses; (b) Irrigation; (c) Farm Yard Manure; (d) Cost of chemical fertilizer; (e) Leaf harvest and f) Miscelleneous;

Tables 6.3 Recurring expenditure on one acre of established irrigated mulberry garden from second year onwards

Sl. No.	*Particulars*	*Mandays (Qty)*			*Rate per manday (Rs.)*		*Amount (Rs.)*	
(a)	Cultivation expenses	Family labour 45	Hired 20	Total 65	350	Family labour 15,750	Hired 7000	Total 22,750
(b)	Irrigation Farm yard manure	-	-	-	-	-	-	-
(c)	Cost of chemical fertilizer	-	-	-	-	-	-	-
(d)	Leaf harvest	-	-	-	-	-	-	-
(e)	Miscelleneous	40	15	55	350	14,000	5250	19,250
(f)		-	-	-			1000	1000
	Total	**85**	**25**	**120**		**29,750**	**17,250**	**43,000**

Source: Field Data.

(a) Cultivation expenses– As mentioned earlier, the rearing of silkworms involves cultivation of mulberry trees, which provide a regular supply of leaves. The success of good quality cocoon yield totally depends upon proper planning and maintenance of mulberry garden / plant and cultivation is a crucial process. It is evident from Table 6.3, that the farmers incurred the highest expenditure on the process of cultivation, this may be attributed to the fact that the number of mandays involved in cultivation is the most (55 percent) as compared to other activities. The total cost of cultivation is estimated at Rs.22,750. As shown in Table 5.3 out of the total 65 days required a significant share (45 days) is contributed by family labour which reduces the cost of labour considerably and the actual expenditure incurred on hired labour for cultivation was Rs.7000 (31 percent).

(b) Irrigation– Saitual cluster is also endowed by nature with congenial climate for sericulture which reduces the dependence on irrigation facilities considerably for growing mulberry. The researcher observed that the mulberry farms in Saitual cluster were rain-fed and none of the agripreneurs depended on irrigation facilities. This is reflected on the cost of irrigation facilities estimated to be NIL.

(c) Farm Yard Manure– As shown in Table 6.3, the cost incurred on Farm Yard Manure is nil since the soil of Mizoram is naturally suitable to grow a healthy mulberry garden without the help of manure. All the farmers in Saitual cluster are dependent on organic farming.

(d) Cost of chemical fertilizer– Notably all the farmers in Saitual followed organic farming which reduced the cost considerably. As shown in Table 6.3, none of the agripreneurs were treating their land with fertilizers therefore expenditure on fertilizers is also nil.

(e) Leaf harvest– Silkworms feed on mulberry leaves. The success of silkworm rearing depends on the quality of leaf that is fed to silk worms. Silkworms prefer fresh, healthy mulberry leaves. Silkworms during different stages prefer different nutritive quality of leaves. Harvesting of mulberry leaves from the mulberry garden include (a) Leaf picking, (b) shoot-harvest, (c) branch cutting. Leaves harvested depends on the type of rearing method adopted. The first leaf harvest is usually done after 8 months of planting. In Saitual cluster the farmers harvest leaves five times in a year which required a total mandays of 55 as shown in table 6.3. The value of leaf harvesting is around Rs. 19250, however, the actual expenses incurred on hired labour was Rs.5,250.

The total cost of recurring expenditure on one acre of established irrigated mulberry garden from second year onwards was Rs.43,000 including miscellaneous expenditure. However, the actual expenses on hired labour is Rs. 13,250. It is evident that the expenditure is reduced considerably due to the involvement of family labour. In a similar study conducted by Rani (2006) in Anantapur district the cost incurred for application of Farm Yard Manure (FYM) and Chemical fertilizer is Rs.3,870 which is nil in Saitual. Hence, the recurring expenditure on one acre of established garden is considerably lower in Saitual.

Table 6.4 – Estimated Actual Expenditure Incurred on Maintenance of One Acre irrigated Mulberry Garden

Sl. No.	*Particulars*	*Upto 1*	*1 to 2*	*> 2*
1.	Cultivation:-			
(a)	Human Labour (hired only)			
	(i) Cultivation (20 md x350)	7000	14,000	21,000
	(ii) Leaf harvesting (15 md x350)	5,250	10,500	15,750
(b)	Bullock Labour	-	-	-
2.	FYM	-	-	-
3.	Chemical fertilisers	-	-	-
4.	Non-recurring	-	-	-
5.	Miscellaneous	1000	2000	3000
	Total	**13,250**	**26,500**	**39,750**

Source: Field Data md = Mandays.

Note: Family labour not included in estimated cost.

Table 6.4 gives a snap shot of the expenditure incurred by small, medium and large farmers in Saitual. It shows the estimated expenditure incurred by the sericulturists of different size groups which varies from Rs.13,250 to 39,750. As mentioned earlier, the farmers incurred an expenditure of Rs.13,250 (31 percent) of the estimated cost (Rs.43,000) for maintenance of one acre irrigated mulberry garden. The mulberry plantation is fully established in one year and reaches its maximum yield from the second year onwards under irrigated conditions. The leaf yield was more or less uniform in all the seasons in the seasons in the irrigated mulberry farms in Saitual cluster.

II. Silkworm Rearing

The researcher has further estimated the quantity of silkworms reared per household.

Table – 6.5 Quantity of silk worms reared per household for 200 dfls

Size of Mulberry Landholdings Group (in Acre)	*Average Quantity reared per crop*	*Average No. of rearings*	*Annual quantity (in kgs)*
Upto 1	120 kgs	5	600
1 to 2	240 kgs	5	1,200
>2	360 kgs	5	1,800

Source: Field Data.

The rearing starts with the purchase of silkworm eggs called disease – free-layings (dfls) or industrial seed normally at the cost of Rs250 per hundred dfls. Sericulturists usually buy these eggs from government grainages or licensed seed-producers (Rani, 2006). In other words, worms are introduced through DFLs (Disease Free Layings, i.e. eggs). In Saitual cluster the dfls were supplied by the government according to the requirements of the farmers. For one acre of mulberry garden around 200 dfls were reared in Saitual. Normally, for one acre of land the weight of cocoons obtained from 100 dfls is around 50-70 kgs of cocoons which are produced with an average number of rearing between 4 to 5 times in a year. On an average all the sericulturists harvest five crops per year. From table 6.5, it is evident that the annual production of silkworm from 200 dfls for mulberry size of one acre is around 600 kgs. In other words, the annual production of cocoons for one acre is estimated at 600 kgs of cocoons whereas for a landholding of 2 acres it is estimated to be 1200 kgs and 1800 kgs respectively.

It is pertinent to note that organic farming is enabling the agripreneurs in Saitual to produce 600 kgs of cocoons which compares favourably to cocoon production in Erode district of Tamil Nadu where the average cocoon production was 805.62 kgs on average from one acre in a year (Prakasam, 2014) The farmers here incurred a cost of Rs. 7076.87 for fertilizers and Rs. 3576.87 annually per acre per year on plant protection chemicals whereas no such fertilizers or plant protection chemicals were used to mulberry leaves in Saitual cluster. However, in a study conducted in Murshidabad, West Bengal revealed that 900 kgs of cocoons were produced per acre/year (Trivedi & Sarkar, 2015).

The success of sericulture in Saitual can become a role model for other states to follow and emulate. Organic farming retards degradation of land and enables longevity of fertility of the land.

Table – 6.6: Expenditure involved in Rearing of 100 dfls in a year.

Sl. no	*Description*	*Mandays*	
1.	Cost of dfls (a) Rs. Per 100 dfls	-	NIL
2.	Cost of Labour wage (a) First & Second Instar (b) Third Instar (c) Fourth Instar (d) Fifth Instar (e) Collection of ripend worm and mounting	 - 12 16 20 -	 - 720 960 1,200
3.	Paraffin paper formalin, news paper Transportation charges etc	-	
	Total		**2,520**

Source: Field Data.
Note: Wages paid at Rs.60 per manday

Silkworm passes through four distinct stages egg, larva, pupa and adult during its life cycle. The duration of life cycle may usually lasts 6-8 weeks depending upon racial characteristics and climatic conditions (Mahesha, 2008). These stages can also be classified as First Instar to Fifth Instar. As seen in the table 6.6, from the Third Instar to fifth instar labour are employed by the farmers at the rate of Rs.60 per manday. Due to the delicate nature of the silkworms, the rearing activity demands utmost care and skill during these stages. Hence, sericulturists have to depend on skilled labour. The rearing activity is labour intensive and accordingly the estimated expenditure on the labour component is also higher than the other inputs involved in this activity. The involvement of family labour considerably reduces the expenditure on labour. Table 6.6 shows the average expenditure incurred by farmers on hired workers in a year and on an average the cost involved for rearing of 150 dfls works out to be Rs.2,520. The dfls are provided by the government therefore the expenses is nil throughout the year.

Table – 6.7 Expenditure incurred on rearing in a year (in Rs.)

Particulars	
Cost of dfls reared	-
Expenditure on labour	2,520
Miscellaneous	1000
Total	**3520**

Source: Field Data.

Table 6.7 shows the expenditure incurred on rearing in a year for one acre mulberry size. As mentioned earlier, the cost of dfls is nil since the government is supplying the dfls to the farmers.

The expenditure on labour is Rs.2,520 (refer table 6.7). The miscellaneous expenditure is estimated to be Rs. 1000, the miscellaneous may include the expenses of farmers on purchasing extra plastic trays, sprayer, net, disinfectant as per their requirements. As mentioned earlier in table 6.2 almost all of the rearing equipment are provided by the government however, sometimes the farmers are faced with the need of buying extra rearing equipment other than the ones supplied by the government.

Accordingly, the total expenditure incurred on rearing in a years is estimated as Rs.3,520.

Table 6.8 Economics of Silkwrom Rearing in One Acre of Mulberry Plantation

Particulars	*Quantity*
No. of crop per year	5 times
No. of dfls to be reared per crop	200 nos.
No. of dfls reared in a year	1000 nos.
Quantity of cocoon per 100 dfls	60 kgs
Quantity of cocoon per 200 dfls	120 kgs
Production of cocoon per year	600 kgs
Annual income from sale of 600 Kgs cocoons @200 per kg	Rs.1,20,000

Source: Field Data.

Table 6.8 shows the annual income earned by the sericulturists from one acre of mulberry plantation. In Saitual cluster, around 200 dfls were reared per crop in on acre of mulberry and the total no. of crop per year is 5 times. As seen in Table 6.8, 1000 nos. of dfls were reared in year in one acre of mulberry. As mentioned earlier, worms are introduced through DFLs (Disease Free Layings, i.e. eggs). In Saitual cluster the dfls were supplied by the government according to the requirements of the farmers. For one acre of mulberry garden around 200 dfls were reared in Saitual. Normally, for one acre of land the weight of cocoons obtained from 100 dfls is around 50-70 kgs of cocoons which are produced with an average number of rearing between 4 to 5 times in a year and the quantity of cocoon produced per 100 are 60 kgs, hence, the total production of cocoon in year was estimated at 600 kgs. As mentioned earlier, the farmers sell these cocoons to the Cocoon collection centre in Saitual where the cocoons are dried and weighted and categorized into different grades according to their weights. The rates of the cocoons differ according to the category it falls under.

The average rate of the cocoons in Saitual cluster was around Rs.200 per kgs. It is evident from Table 6.8 that with a total production 600 kgs of cocoons in a year the annual income from silkworm rearing in one acre of mulberry plantation was estimated at Rs. 1,20,000.

Table – 6.9: Costs and returns on one acre of irrigated mulberry garden

Sl. No.	*Particulars*	*Rs.*
A.	Expenditure (a) Production of mulberry leaf (b) Silkworm rearing (c) Total	13,250 3520 16,770 600 kgs
B.	Quantity of cocoons produced (in kgs)	1,20,000
C.	Returns in Rs. Through sale of cocoon at Rs.200/ per kg	1,03,230
D.	Net Returns (in Rs.)	

Source: Field Data.

As mentioned earlier, the success of sericulture enterprise depends on the level of profits it enjoys. The returns obtained by sericulturists act as a measure in determining the economic viability of sericulture activity. Therefore an attempt is made to analyse the cost and net returns from the sericulture enterprise in the study area. Table 6.9 gives a clear picture of the costs and returns on one acre of irrigated mulberry garden. It is evident from the Table 6.9 that the total expenditure is Rs.16, 770 during the year. The quantity of cocoon produced on an average for 100 dfls is 60 kgs of cocoon and average number of rearing is 5 times, hence, around 600 kgs of cocoons are produced in a year.

After rearing of silkworms and obtaining cocoon, the next major activity is taking them to markets for selling. Sericulturists usually prefer to take them to nearby markerts to reduce the percentage of damage and transport costs. Sericulturists in Saitual cluster sells their cocoons to the Cocoon Purchasing Centre which is located in Saitual. This centre is established by the government to make it convenient for the farmars of the cluster to sell their cocoons.

In the purchasing centre the cocoons are dried and then weighed by using weighing device. Based on the weight of the cocoon, the cocoon are categorized into four grade A, B, C and D. A grade being the highest quality followed B and so on and so forth. The rates of the cocoons were fixed by the government based on their grade.

It is clear from Table 6.9 that the amount of returns through sale of cocoon is Rs. 1,20,000 in a year. However, after deducting all the expenditure incurred the net returns is Rs.1,03,230 for one acre of mulberry land. In a study conducted by Rani (2006) in Anantapur district the net returns is Rs. 30,045 for acre of mulberry land, which is lesser.

This maybe attributed to the fact that the expenditure incurred by the farmers in this cluster is lesser as the farmers do not have to incur expenses on factors such as Farm Yard Manure (FYM), Chemical fertilizers, irrigation facilities and rearing appliances. As mentioned earlier, the 80 percent of the rearing appliances are sanctioned by the government.

A comparison with the yield in Anantarpur District of Andhra Pradesh shows that the average production of cocoons from one acre by rearing 300 dfls was 119.65 per crop with a net return of Rs. 39,134 (Rani J, 2007) while in Saitual cluster by rearing 200 dfls in one acre the average production of cocoons was 120 per crop (Table 4.10) with a net return of Rs. 1, 03,230.

It is evident that sericulture has emerged as a successful economic activity giving remarkable returns to the agripreneurs. Rs. 1,20,000 is the return that accrues to the farmers having a land holding of one acre whereas it may be estimated to be Rs. 2,40,000 for two acres and Rs. 3,60,000 for more than two acres. It was observed that the maximum land holding in Saitual was 5 acres with most of the large farmers (54) having a land holding of 3 acres.

2. Conclusion

Sericulture has emerged as a sustainable livelihood option in Saitual cluster giving remarkable returns to the agripreneurs in the cluster. Moreover, the cluster development initiative of the Government of Mizoram has provided an impetus to the business by means of subsidy in terms of providing rearing infrastructure in the form of construction of rearing house and supply of rearing equipments and NLUP. This has lowered the actual cost incurred by the agripreneurs per acre to Rs.49,500. The total expenditure incurred on one acre of mulberry farm was Rs.16,770 and the returns that accrued to the agripreneurs was Rs.1,20,000. The net returns for the agripreneur per acre/year was estimated at Rs.1,03,230. It is evident that sericulture was giving remarkable returns to the agripreneurs. Sustained cluster development initiatives by the Government of Mizoram will ensure the success of prosperity of this industry in Mizoram.

References

Central Silk Board. (2015). Intensive Bivoltine Sericulture Technology Package, Central Sericultural Research & Training Institure (IS0 9001: 2015 Certified), Govt. of India: Ministry of Textiles, West Bengal.

CSRTI. (2005). Disinfection and Hygiene in Silkworm Rearing, Central Sericultural Research & Training Institute (ISO 9001: 2015 Certified), Central Silk Board, Ministry of Textiles, Govt. of India, Srirampura.

Hanumappa, H.G., & Erappa, S. (1985). Economic issues in sericulture: study of Karnataka. *Economic and Political Weekly* 20(31), 3122-3224.

Rani, J.U. (2007). Employment Generation to Women in Drought Prone Areas:A Study With Reference to the Development of Sericulture in Anantapur District of Andhra Pradesh. *Journal of Social Sciences*, 14(3), 249-255.

Krishnaswami, D.N.S. (1986). Mulberry Cultivation in South India, Central Sericultural Research & Training lnstitute, Mysore, Published by: Shri V. Balasubramanian, lAS, Member-Secretary Central Silk Board United Mansions No. 39, Bangalore.

Mahesha, H.B.Dr. (2008). Life Cycle of Bombyx mori, Mysore. Retrieved From: http://hbmahesh.weebly.com/uploads/3/4/2/2/3422804/3.life_cyclemorphology_of_b._mori-o_e_word_13-14.pdf

Prakasam, K., & Ravi, G. Dr. (2014). Sericulture-An Ideal Enterprise for Sustainable Income in Erode District of Tamil Nadu. *Language in India*, ISSN 1930-2940, Vol. 14, No. 9.

Rani, G.S. (2006). Women in Sericulture, ISBN 81-81-8356-098-9, Discovery Publishing House, New Delhi.

Trivedi, S., & Sarkar, K. (2015). Comparative study on income generation through agriculture crop and sericulture at farmer's level in Murshidabad district. *Journal of Entomology and Zoology Studies*, 3(1), 242-245.

Chapter - 7

Conclusion and Suggesstions

This last chapter summarizes the study and gives suggestions for the sustenance and growth of the cluster.Entrepreneurship is a necessary ingredient for stimulating economic growth and employment opportunities in all societies. Entrepreneurial activities differ substantially depending on the type of organization and creativity involved. It may pertain to agriculture, industry, trade or other professions. In the developing world, successful small businesses are the primary engines of job creation, income growth, and poverty reduction.

Sericulture is a largely village-based industry providing employment opportunities to a large section of the rural population in India. Sericulture, or silk farming, is the rearing of silkworms for the production of silk. It is an agro-based industry and has a very short gestation period, having the potential to generate adequate returns from even small areas of land. Sericulture has the potential to provide gainful self-employment to farmer households in rural areas (Government of India, 2013).

1. Introduction

Chapter 1 presents a conceptual framework of clusters and cluster development with a focus on sericulture. The chapter presents an overview of silk industry globally and in India and examines its significance to the Indian economy in terms of production of silk, employment, exports and so on.

Indian silk industry is an integral part of the Indian textile industry and is among the oldest industries in India. It engages around 60 lakh workers and it involves small and marginal farmers. Mulberry, Tasar, Muga and Eri are the types of silk produced in the Indian silk industry. Indian silk industry is the second highest contribution of silk to the world production. Consistent market demand and remarkable approach has led to the widening of this industry (Bhushi and Pharsiyawar, 2004). The Raw Silk Production of India was 31,906 MT in 2017-18.China is the largest producer of raw silk followed by India and Brazil. (CSB, 2018).

Karnataka was the largest producer of Raw Silk in India with a total production of 11592 MT in 2018-19 followed by Andhra Pradesh with a total production of 7481 MT in 2018-19. Some of the other leading producers of raw silk in India include Telangana, Tamil Nadu, Kerala and Maharashtra. Among the seven sisters of North-east India viz., Arunachal Pradesh, Assam, Meghalaya, Manipur, Mizoram, Nagaland and Tripura, Assam is the leading producer of silk with 5029 MT in 2018-19. Mizoram is one of the leading producers among the North-east state with total production of 92 MT in 2018-19. The production of raw silk in Mizoram is showing an increasing trend from 64 MT in 2015-16 to 92 MT in 2018-19 (CSB, 2018). The export earnings during 2017-18 were Rs. 1,649.48 crores (CSB, 2019). Sericulture is an agro based activity which offers immense avenues for employment generation in India. This may be attributed to the fact that it is highly labour intensive industry providing high returns to the sericulturists. Sericulture is a highly profitable activity and its profitability depends on the production of quality mulberry leaves and its conversion into quality cocoons at economic costs. Sericulture plays a vital role in rural development, as it integrates well with the farming systems and has the potential to generate attractive income throughout the year. It needs low capital and provides year round employment (Hanumappa and Erappa, 1985). In view of this, it is imperative to understand the economics of sericulture and estimate the returns that accrue to the sericulturists in Saitual.

Over the years sericulture is playing a vital role in development of the rural economy of Mizoram, in terms of employment opportunities. Mizoram occupies the 17th place in respect of area under mulberry, cocoon and silk raw production in India during 2011-2012 (Rathnam, Narasaiah and Murthy, 2013).

The economy of Saitual is basically agrarian in nature and the major agricultural crops grown are corn, sugarcane and vegetables. Sericulture has become an important occupation in recent years after the cluster started taking its shape in 2009. As mentioned earlier, Saitual has been identified as one among 10 sericulture clusters in Mizoram. The cluster is an ideal place for taking up sericulture activities with vast tracts of land under cultivation of mulberry leaves.

"Cluster Promotion Programme" (CPP) was launched by Central Silk Board and implemented during XI plan jointly with state sericulture departments organizing 50 sericulture clusters covering both mulberry and *Vanya*sectors spread over 17 states for the promotion of sericulture especially the bivoltine.

In pursuance of the suggestion from the Planning Commission and Ministry of Textiles, Government of India, Central Silk Board (CSB) and Departments of Sericulture (DOS) of selected states has initiated Cluster Promotion Programme during 2007-12. The CBS and DOS have jointly identified 45 model sericulture clusters in pre-cocoon sector during 2008-09 and 2009-10, in 16 States including Mizoram. The sericulture department of Mizoram selected 10 clusters under the 'Cluster area development project' namely Khamrang, Saitual, Darlung, Kanghmun, Khawhai, Serchhip, Zobawk, Rotlang, Bawktlang and Lungbun as on 2011-12 (Directorate of Sericulture, Government of Mizoram, 2012).

With the joint concentrated efforts, 5874 MTs of Bivoltine raw silk has been produced against Country's target of 6200 MTs during 2017-18 (11.5 % increase over 5266 MT produced in 2016-17). Bivoltine clusters contributed 4100 MT (70.0%) out of the country's total BV raw silk production of 5874MT. During 2018-19 the total BV raw silk production stands at 6911 MT out of which 151 clusters contributed 4987 MT (72.16%).(CSB, 2019).

The present study has explored various facets of agripreneurship in Saitual Sericulture cluster, located in the tribal state of Mizoram in North East India viz; the socioeconomic profile of the agripreneurs, the motivational factors that influenced their decision to become entrepreneurs, the role of cluster processes in entrepreneurship development in Saitual cluster. The study also evaluated the financial performance of the agri-enterprises in the cluster and gives suggestions for the sustenance and growth of the enterprises in the cluster.

2. The Present Study

This chapter focuses on the research problem. The need for the study, the statement of the problem, a review of relevant literature, the research design which include the objectives of the study and the methodology of the study are clearly spelt out in this chapter. The review of literature covered the areas of entrepreneurship, agripreneurship, cluster development and sericulture to understand the gap in research. The specific objectives of the present study are to study the socio-economic profile of agripreneurs of the sericulture cluster, to ascertain the motivational factors of the agripreneurs, to analyse the impact of cluster on entrepreneurship development in the cluster, to assess the performance of the sericulture enterprises and to offer suitable suggestions to the agrienterprises in the cluster. The study was conducted in Saitual Cluster village, located at about 77 kilometers from Aizawl, the capital city of Mizoram. For the purpose of the present study, an agripreneur is any person who is engaged in rearing of silkworms on a commercial basis. The present study relies on the primary as well as secondary data. The primary data was collected through a structured questionnaire, administered to all agripreneurs (180 in number) engaged in sericulture in Saitual cluster during December 2016 to February 2017. The secondary data was collected by consulting relevant reports, journals, books, bulletins and websites.

Simple statistical devices such as percentages and averages wherever relevant were used to interpret and analyse data collected. Factors motivating and facilitating entrepreneurship were rated by weighted scores. The data collected was also analysed by using statistical tools called SPSS. Kruskal-Wallis test was used to find whether there was any significant relationship between the motivation factors among the different group of farmers.

3. Socio-economic Characteristics of Entrepreneurs

The socioeconomic milieu plays an important role in the emergence and development of entrepreneurs as they are embedded in socioeconomic systems. The researcher exploredthe socioeconomic characteristics, viz age, gender, educational qualifications, family structure, family size, occupation, year of commencement of business, marital status, age-sex distribution etc. of the entrepreneurs in Saitual cluster.

Saitual cluster started to take its form in 1994 with one farmer engaging in sericulture for commercial purposes. The period between 2009-14 witnessed the birth of maximum number of units (137 units). This period coincided with the launching of the 'Cluster area development project' including Saitual cluster as on 2011-2012 (Directorate of Sericulture, Government of Mizoram, 2012) along with the initiatives taken by the Government through the scheme New Land Use Policy (NLUP). New Land Use Policy (NLUP) initiated on 14th January, 2011. 76 percent of the farmers in Saitual were males and 23.9 percent of females. Out of the180 agripreneurs, a significant number of the farmers were in the age group of 4150 years (47 percent), followed by the age group of 31-40 years (46 percent) and farmers who were above 60 years of age (37 percent).

35 percent of the farmer was in the age group of 51-60 and only 15 farmers (8.3 percent) were below 30 years of age. It is evident that there is no barrier of age in the cluster and the different activities of sericulture is suitable for all age groups.

All the respondents were Mizos (*Assam–Burman sub-groups*[2] of the Tibeto Chinese race). It was also observed that none of the farmers belonged to the neighbouring country, Myanmar as is commonly observed in other parts of Mizoram such as Aizawl and Lunglei. All the respondents belonged to the ST category.

As the majority (87%) of Mizos are Christians in various denominations, interestingly all the farmers in the Saitual cluster were Christians. A high proportion (76.7 percent) of the sample entrepreneurs in this cluster live in a nuclear family structure.

The Mizos are comprised of different tribes, sub tribes and clans. The state of Mizoram is inhabited by a number of tribes which may be broadly divided into nine major and thirteen minor tribes and sub- tribes (Verghese and Thanzawna 1997). Twenty different tribes or sub-tribes or clans were involved in the commercial production of cocoons in the cluster. It is observed that the sample entrepreneurs in Saitual cluster share a strong sense of common identity despite the fact that they belonged to different tribes or sub-tribes or clans and abound in 'social capital.'

A glimpse into the classification of farm holdings shows that the size for mulberry land holdings in the study area varies from 0.5 acres to 3 acres. 22.22 percent of farmers practicing sericulture in the cluster ownedless than one acre and 47.8 percent farmers owned one to two acres and around 30 percent farmers owned above two acres.

A majority of farmers i.e. 162 (90 percent) in Saitual cluster were educated up to school level and only 10 farmers (5.6 percent) have collegiate education. There were 8 farmers who are illiterate. It also suggests that the the Saitual sericulture cluster compared favourably in the literacy rate with the literacy level of Mizoram.

An enquiry into the marital status of the agripreneurs shows that 84.4 percent of the sample entrepreneurs were married and 6.1 percent of the entrepreneurs were unmarried, while about 10 percent of the respondents were widows or divorced.All the farmers in the Saitual cluster were Christians. A high proportion (76.7 percent) of the sample entrepreneurs in this cluster lives separately, only 23.3 percent of the entrepreneurs were still living with parents. Majority of the farmers i.e. 58.3 percent of the sample beneficiary households had family size below five members and followed by farmers belonging to 6-10 members of family (40.6 percent). It can be said that sericulture activity is not confined to those households who have large number of family members.

Most of the entrepreneurs (61.7 percent) were natives of Saitual. Around 38.3 percent of the respondents have migrated to Saitual cluster from other places in Mizoram.Out of the total entrepreneurs who have migrated from other places in Mizoram to Saitual cluster, a majority of 44 farmers have migrated in search of better opportunities for employment.

It was further observed that 77.3 percent of the entrepreneurs were solely dependent on sericulture. Only 8.9 percent of the entrepreneurs considered business as their main occupation and for 11 entrepreneurs, Government's job was the main occupation. Notably, sericulture has emerged as an important occupation providing livelihood to the farmers in the cluster.

An analysis of income earned by the entrepreneurs from all sources showed that majority of the farmers (34 %) earn above Rs.2,00,000 and 53 farmers (29 %) earn between Rs.1,50,00 – Rs. 2,00,000 and around 27 percent of the farmers earn between Rs.1,00,000 and Rs.1,50,000. Only 17 farmers earn below Rs.1, 00,000. It was further observed that majority of the farmers (30 percent) earn above Rs.2, 00,000 annually solely from sericulture activity.Around 26 percent (46) of the farmers earn between Rs.1, 50,000 to Rs. 2,00,000 and around 22 percent (40) of the farmers earn Rs.100,000 to Rs.1,50,000. The remaining 40 farmers (22 percent) earn below Rs. 1, 00,000. Sericulture has emerged as a significant source of employment and a sustainable livelihood option for the farmers of Saitual cluster.

4. Role of Cluster in Entrepreneurship Development

Clustering of firms sets into motion several advantages that create a spin-off of enterprises in the cluster. As observed by Nadvi and Barrientos (2004), clustering sets into motion of range of potential benefits which can be through externality gains, joint action, and local social capital. Clusters can set into motion processes that improve the ability of small firms to improve market across through externality gains through joint action. This can raise incomes for those who work in clusters, raise their assets and capabilities and have a significant impact on lowering levels of poverty and social deprivation.

This chapter investigated the impact of cluster on entrepreneurship development. To achieve this objective, the researcher attempted to assess the extent of influence exerted by the cluster on entrepreneurship in matters such as initial expectations of agripreneurs from support agencies, agripreneurs economic reasons for entering the sericulture industry and agripreneurs reasons for establishing their units in Saitual cluster.

The agripreneurs were asked to accord ranks to their reasons wherever needed in order of their importance. These reasons were subsequently rated by weighted score to recognize their underlying importance on the emergence of entrepreneurship in the cluster.

The present study identified the initial expectations of the agripreneurs at the time of commencement of their enterprise in Saitual cluster. It is observed that availability of land was the dominant expectation of the agripreneurs at the time of starting their venture. Entrepreneurship has sprung in Saitual cluster as an outcome of the primary expectation of utilizing land for sericulture activities. Land is the most important requirement for practicing sericulture farming, for from it food for silkworms will be harvested. The agrobased sericulture begins with land related activities to grow silkworm.

It is further observed that 'utilization of available ;land for growing mulberry' of land has been accorded the highest rating of 33.06 percent followed by 'suitable climate' accorded second rank with a rating of 32.78 percent and 'assistance from government' has been assigned the third rank with a rating of 28.24 percent.

Further the present study also sought a self-assessment of the fulfilment of the agripreneurs initial expectations. It is observed that 66.67 percent of the agripreneurs seem to have achieved fulfilment of their expectations, where 17.77 percent of the agripreneurs expressed discontent with their initial expectations.

The present study has also attempted to examine the reasons behind the entry of agripreneurs into sericulture. It is observed that the highest rating was accorded to the reason,'Easy to establish mulberry garden' (32.96 percent) followed by 'ownership of agriculture land' (28.80 percent) and ' involvement of family labour' (16.11 percent).

The present study also enquired into the probable reasons behind the agripreneurs establishing his or her unit in the cluster to gain an insight into the role played by cluster processes on the emergence of entrepreneurship in Saitual.

The highest rating (1st rank) was accorded to availability of land in the cluster (43.06 percent), followed by nearness to cocoon purchasing centre having accorded the 2nd rank (19.35 percent) and government support and assistance was accorded the 3rd rank (14.17 percent).Existence of similar units in the cluster' was ranked 4th with a rating of only 4.91 percent followed by other reasons.

The present study also enquired into the agripreneur's alternate proposals had there been no cluster in Saitual in order to gauge the magnitude of the desire for taking up any entrepreneurial ventures.75 (41.67 percent) agripreneurs out of 180 indicated that they were uncertain about their second opinion, as they cited 'can't say'. However, 51 (28.33 percent) of them would take up a new job while 24 (13.33 percent) of them will set up the samesericulture business elsewhere. Only 7.22 percent would like to take up sericulture had there been no cluster in Saitual meanwhile 8 percent of the agripreneurs indicated that they would not enter the same business.

The present study also examined the level of satisfaction of the farmers with the common facilities available to them in the cluster provided by the Sericulture department of Mizoram. As the table shows majority of the farmers i.e 104 farmers out of the 180 are satisfied with the facilities provided to them by the government.However, 57 of them are not satisfied by the facilities provided by the government in the cluster.

5. Motivational Factors for Agripreneurship in Saitual Cluster

In order to have a full understanding of the role of motivation in the overall process of entrepreneurship in Saitual cluster, this chapter has enquired into entrepreneurial motivations such as entrepreneurial ambitions, reasons compelling entrepreneurs to enter the industry, factors facilitating their entry into entrepreneurship, entrepreneurs expectations and the degree of fulfillment of their expectations and reasons for setting up their unit in this cluster. The study also enquired into whether they would like their children to continue as entrepreneurs in the same industry, the entrepreneur's satisfaction level with common facilities available in the cluster.

The present study has identified several motivational factors that could have led to entrepreneurship in the cluster viz. 'to earn a livelihood', 'to get employment', 'to give financial security to my family (Necessity Motives) ; 'to gain independence', 'to gain social prestige', 'Enjoyment of the work' (Independent Motives); 'to earn money'; 'to make use of idle funds'; 'to diversify my economic interests', 'influenced by the success stories of other entrepreneurs' (Increase-wealth motives). Necessity motive indicates participation in entrepreneurial activity primarily because they have no other options for work whereas independence motive indicates the need for entrepreneurs to gain independence.

Mean scores measured on a 5 point scale are used (Khanka 2009) to assess the motivational factors of small agripreneurs are farmers who own less than one acre of land, medium who own 1-2 acres of land and large agripreneurs are those who own more than 2 acres of land. Further in order to get a clear understanding of the motives that drive these agripreneurs, Kruskal Wallis (H Test) was used to identify various motives to small and medium and large farmers. The research has attempted to understand whether there is a variation in motives that drives entrepreneurial aspirations of these farmers on the basis of their land holdings. Accordingly, hypotheses were framed to test each motivational factor on the basis of land holding of the agripreneurs classified as small, medium and large.

'Making money' emerged as the most significant motivational factor for the farmer entrepreneur (with a mean score of 4.2) in Saitual. The null hypothesis H_0: There is no significant relationship between the size of the farm holding and the motive 'To earn money' was rejected which shows that there is a significant relationship between the size of the farm holding and the motive 'To earn a livelihood.'

To examine the relationship further, analysis has been done on different group of farmers – 'small and medium farmers' and 'medium and large farmers'. Interestingly the hypothesis Ho: There is no significant relationship between small and medium farmers and the motive 'To earn money' was rejected. It is evident that the motive 'to earn money' has played a dominant role in the entrepreneurial aspirations of the large farmers. The null hypothesis 'Ho: There is no significant relationship between medium and large farmers and the motive 'To earn money' was failed to be rejected which shows that therefore conclude that there is no significant relationship between medium and large farmers and the motive 'To earn money'

'Earning a livelihood' emerged as the second most important entrepreneurial motive of the agripreneurs in Saitual Cluster with the score of 4.1. Further, the hypothesis 'Ho: There is no significant relationship between the size of the farm holding and the motive 'to earn a a livelihood' was rejected, which clearly shows that all the agripreneurs considered sericulture as a livelihood option irrespective of the land holding.

Financial security emerged as another significant motivating factor for farmers to enter the industry with a mean of 4.0 and the motive 'Enjoying the work' was accorded the fourth rank by the farmer entrepreneurs with a mean of 3.89.

'Gaining independence' has not emerged as a significant motive for the agripreneurs with a mean score of only 3.87. Diversifying economic interest has been accorded a mean score of 3.86 by the agripreneurs. 'Influenced by the success stories of other entrepreneurs' was accorded the sixth rank by the agripreneurs with a mean score of 3.12.

It appears that for the farmers in Saitual unemployment was not the primary factor that led them to participate in Sericulture since this motive was accorded only 2.58 mean score. Gaining social prestige is not a significant motive for the farmers having accorded a mean score of only 2.5. Making use of idle funds is not a significant motive for the farmers having accorded the least mean score of 1.96.

The study also enquired into what aspiration sericulture holds for the entrepreneurs for their next generation.The entrepreneurs were asked whether they would like their children to become entrepreneurs in the sericulture industry 65 percent of the entrepreneurs would like their children to become entrepreneurs in the same business whereas about 35 percent of the entrepreneurs (63 in number) do not want their children to become entrepreneurs in sericulture industry.

The present study further elicited answers from 63 entrepreneurs about the reasons behind their not wanting their children to take up entrepreneurship in sericulture. A high majority of the farmers (71.43 percent) feel that their children may not be interested in taking up sericulture as a source of income and 19 percent of the farmers claim that sericulture is not profitable enough for their children to take up.

Notably only 19 percent of the 63 entrepreneurs who feel that children would not be interested in this business perceived non profitability as an entry barrier for the next generation.An overwhelming majority of farmer entrepreneurs are willing to adopt new ideas for the growth of their business.

6. Financial Performance of Sericulture Enterprises

The researcher has further attempted to estimate the financial performance of the agri enterprises in Saitual cluster.

The researcher has estimated the various costs involved in establishment and management of one acre of mulberry garden in Saitual.Sericulture as an economic activity comprises of two main activities:

I. MULBERRY CULTIVATION– which includes *establishment of mulberry garden* (initial stage) and *recurring expenditure from second year onwards;*

II. SILKWORM REARING – which includes *quantity of silkworms reared per household* and *the expenditure involved in rearing;*

The total estimated cost of establishment and management of one acre was Rs.1, 77,260. However, as the farmers have received subsidies in the form of rearing Rs. 77,760 and Rs.50,000 under NLUP scheme from the Government of Mizoram, the actual cost incurred was Rs. 49,500.

The sericulture farmer incurs a significant expenditure in the first year of establishing expenditure. Thereafter, the agripreneur incurs only the recurring expenditure which have been examined by the researcher. Recurring expenditure on rearing broadly includes (a) Cultivation expenses; (b) Irrigation; (c) Farm Yard Manure; (d) Cost of chemical fertilizer; (e) Leaf harvest and (f) Miscelleneous;

The farmers incurred the highest expenditure on the process of cultivation, this may be attributed to the fact that the number of man days involved in cultivation is the most (55 percent) as compared to other activities. The total cost of cultivation is estimated at Rs. 22,750. As shown in Table 6.3 out of the total 65 days required a significant share (45 days) is contributed by family labour which reduces the cost of labour considerably and the actual expenditure incurred on hired labour for cultivation was Rs. 7000 (31 percent).

The cost incurred on Farm Yard Manure and Cost of chemical fertilizer is nil.

The cost of leaf harvesting was around Rs. 19250 which includes family and hired labour. However, the actual expenses incurred on hired labour was Rs. 5,250.

The total cost of recurring expenditure on one acre of established irrigated mulberry garden from second year onwards was Rs. 43,000 including miscellaneous expenditure.

However, the actual expenses on hired labour is Rs. 13,250

The researcher has further estimated the quantity of silkworms reared per household.The rearing starts with the purchase of silkworm eggs called disease –freelayings (dfls) or industrial seed normally a the cost of Rs250 per hundred dfls. Sericulturists usually buy these eggs from government grainages or licensed seedproducers (Rani, 2006). In other words, worms are introduced through DFLs (Disease Free Layings, i.e. eggs). In Saitual cluster the dfls were supplied by the government according to the requirements of the farmers. For one acre of mulberry garden around

200 dfls were reared in Saitual. Normally, for one acre of land the weight of cocoons obtained from 100 dfls is around 50-70 kgs of cocoons which are produced with an average number of rearing between 4 to 5 times in a year. On an average all the sericulturists harvest five crops per year. From table 5.5, it is evident that the annual production of silkworm from 200 dfls for mulberry size of one acre is around 600 kgs. In other words, the annual production of cocoons for one acre is estimated at 600 kgs of cocoons whereas for a landholding of 2 acres it is estimated to be 1200 kgs and 1800 kgs respectively.

It is pertinent to note that organic farming is enabling the agripreneurs in Saitual to produce 600 kgs of cocoons which compares favourably to cocoon production in Erode district of Tamil Nadu where the average cocoon production was 804.62 kgs on average from one acre in a year (Prakasam, 2014) The farmers here incurred a cost of Rs. 7076.87 for fertilizers and Rs. 3576.87 annually per acre per year on plant protection chemicals whereas no such fertilizers or plant protection chemicals were used to mulberry leaves in Saitual cluster. However, in a study conducted in Murshidabad, West Bengal revealed that 900 kgs of cocoons were produced per acre/year (Trivedi&Sarkar, 2015).The success of sericulture in Saitual can become a role model for other states to follow and emulate. Organic farming retards degradation of land and enables longevity of fertility of the land.

The expenditure incurred on rearing in a year for one acre mulberry size was also estimated by the researcher. The expenditure on labour is Rs. 2,520. The miscellaneous expenditure is estimated to be Rs. 1000, the miscellaneous may include the expenses of farmers on purchasing extra plastic trays, sprayer, net, disinfectant as per their requirements. The total expenditure incurred on rearing in a years is estimated as Rs. 3, 520.

The annual income earned by the sericulturists from one acre of mulberry plantation. In Saitual cluster, around 200 dfls were reared per crop in on acre of mulberry and the total no. of crop per year is 5 times. 1000 nos. of dfls were reared in year in one acre of mulberry.

The average rate of the cocoons in Saitual cluster was around Rs. 200 per kgs. With a total production 600 kgs of cocoons in a year the annual income from silkworm rearing in one acre of mulberry plantation was estimated at Rs. 1,20,000.

Sericulture has emerged as a sustainable livelihood option in Saitual cluster giving remarkable returns to the agripreneurs in the cluster.

Moreover, the cluster development initiative of the Government of Mizoram has provided an impetus to the business by means of subsidy in terms of providing rearing infrastructure in the form of construction of rearing house and supply of rearing equipments and NLUP. This has lowered the actual cost incurred by the agripreneurs per acre to Rs. 49,500. The total expenditure incurred on one acre of mulberry farm was Rs.16,770 and the returns that accrued to the agripreneurs was Rs. 1,20,000. The net returns for the agripreneur per acre/year was estimated at Rs. 1,03,230.

7. Suggestions

This section gives the summary of suggestions for the agripreneurs and other stake holders such as the government and the facilitating agencies involved in the development of the cluster:-

- Socio capital appears to be abundant in the cluster which can be further nurtured and developed to derive socio-economic benefits to the agripreneurs and the state at large.
- The cluster appears to have become a hub of entrepreneurship founded on the key motivational factors of earning a livelihood, attaining financial security and increasing wealth. These entrepreneurial motivations can be nurtured to create a spin-off of enterprises in the cluster and the state of Mizoram. Saitual has the potential to become a benchmark cluster for others to emulate.
- It is evident that that availability of land and family labour complemented by suitable climate for sericulture along with assistance from the Government were key factors that spurred the agripreneurs to commence sericulture activities in Saitual cluster. Since cluster development initiatives by the Government has played a key role in the emergence of entrepreneurship in the cluster. Cluster development activities initiated by the government as part of the CDP has been an overriding factor as compared to cluster processes in initiating farmers into sericulture in the cluster, sustained efforts should be made by the state government and the central government to handhold and support these agripreneurs.
- It is pertinent to note that organic farming is enabling the agripreneurs in Saitual to produce 600 kgs of cocoons which compares favourably to cocoon production in Erode district of Tamil Nadu where the average cocoon production was 804.62 kgs on average from one acre in a year (Prakasam, 2014) The farmers

here incurred a cost of Rs. 7076.87 for fertilizers and Rs. 3576.87 annually per acre per year on plant protection chemicals whereas no such fertilizers or plant protection chemicals were used to mulberry leaves in Saitual cluster. However, in a study conducted in Murshidabad, West Bengal revealed that 900 kgs of cocoons were produced per acre/year (Trivedi & Sarkar, 2015).The success of sericulture in Saitual can become a role model for other states to follow and emulate. Organic farming retards degradation of land and enables longevity of fertility of the land.

- However, during field study it was observed that some farmers faced the threat of infection of the silkworms which directly impacted the quality of the silkworm. Appropriate training and technology should be provided to the farmers to face this challenge.
- During field study it was observed that no Seri-polyclinics were existing in the cluster. Seri-polyclinics should be established and maintained in Saitual under the CPP with technical and financial assistance from DOS and Central Silk Board.

These units serve as a guidance centre for the day to day problems faced by the farmers in mulberry cultivation and silkworm rearing. The farmers are also imparted training in disease management at CSR&TI, Mysore.

- Further, although for each crop, the chawki worms were supplied to the farmers by the Directorate of Sericulture, Govt. of Mizoram, specialists of sericulture should make regular visit to the farmers at all critical stages and provide technical guidance to the farmers.
- The CPP farmers of Saitual should be sensitized through different extension communication programmes such as training programmes, enlightenment programmes, demonstrations, study tours, field days and farmers meet regularly. This will help them to improve their knowledge and adoption level and ultimately lead to increase the productivity.
- Farmers Field School (FFS) is a platform of "Learning Centre" in the farmers' situation and technology transfer is made through the concept of "Seeing is Believing" and Learning by Doing". It is a farmer to farmer's extension teaching method and helps the farmers who can not undergo training at CSRTI, Mysore. The demonstration and teaching are usually conducted at the lead progressive farmers' garden / rearing house in the village and

facilitate all the nearby farmers to participate in the event. Extension workers and subject matter specialists teach the participants about the sericulture technologies in such programs. The main objectives of FFS is to empower the farmers with knowledge and skills and to make them experts in their own field. One lead farmer who had adopted all the sericulture technologies to harvest successful crop is selected and imparted special training is given by scientists of CSR&TI, Mysore. This farmer sensitizes the other farmers through demonstration. 25-30 sericulturists were benefitted in each session conducted. Audio-visual aids like projectors, DVD players, laptops., materials for demonstration, course materials, charts, teaching materials, refreshment etc. to conduct the training programme are provided for each FFS in a cluster. There is an urgent need to select farmers from Saitual for such training programmes to sensitize other farmers in Saitual.

- With the joint concentrated efforts, 5874 MTs of Bivoltine raw silk has been produced against Country's target of 6200 MTs during 2017-18 (11.5 % increase over 5266 MT produced in 2016-17). Bivoltine clusters contributed 4100 MT (70.0%) out of the country's total BV raw silk production of 5874MT. During 2018-19 the total BV raw silk production stands at 6911 MT out of which 151 clusters contributed 4987 MT (72.16%). Saitual cluster which has been selected under the CPP programme can become a benchmark of organic silk farming for the North eastern region of India and contribute to achieving this national target.
- Lastly, research institutions such as Mizoram University (Departments of Zoology and Horticulture and Medicinal Plants) should proactively be involved in up gradation of the technology of sericulture and provide inputs to the farmers in Saitual.

8. Scope For Further Studies

Further studies on entrepreneurship in rural micro enterprises clusters in the region in the nature of diagnostic studies can be undertaken to have a wider perspective of the economy of the state and the North Eastern Region as a whole and provide inputs to policy makers for chalking out relevant policies and programmes for the development of the region. To be more specific, the prospective researchers interested in entrepreneurship and management of small and micro enterprises may consider the following topics of research:

- Gender participation in sericulture.
- Comparative study between sericulture clusters in Mizoram.
- Comparative studies of sericulture between North Eastern states.
- Comparative study of sericulture with other Agri-activities in Mizoram.
- Comparative study between Mulberry silkworm rearing and other silkworms rearing viz. Muga, Eri and Tasar in North East India.

Appendices

APPENDIX – I: QUESTIONNAIRE (IN ENGLISH)

Questionnaire

(A) Socio economic origins and characteristics

(I) Identification Particulars:

A.1 Name of the entrepreneur ____________________________

A.2 Name and address of the farm with ph No__________________

____

____

A.3 Year of commencement of silkworm rearing ________________

A.4 Age:

(a) Below 30
(b) 31-40
(c) 41-50
(d) 51-60
(e) Above 60

A.5 Sex:

(a) Male
(b) Female

A.6 Educational Qualifications:

(a) Illiterate
(b) School
(c) College
(d) University
(e) Any other (Pl. specify)

A.7 Marital Status

(a) Unmarried
(b) Married
(c) Divorce
(d) Widowed

A.8 Religion and Caste ____________________

A.9 Community/Tribe ___________________________

A.10 Family Structure

(a) Joint
(b) Nuclear

A.11 Family Size

(a) Up to 5
(b) 6-10
(c) 11-15
(d) Above 15

A.12 Native place ____________________________

A.13 If migrated, year of migration _________________

A.14 Reasons for migration:

(a) For silkworm rearing
(b) For economic reasons
(c) Other reasons (Pl specify)

A.15 Main occupation of entrepreneur/entrepreneur's family:

(a) Sericulture
(b) Agriculture/jhumming (other than silkworm rearing)
(c) Business/Trade
(c) Job
(d) Others

A.16 Total family annual income from all sources -

(a) Up to Rs. 20,000
(b) Rs. 20001 – Rs. 40,000
(c) Rs. 40001 – Rs. 60,000
(d) Rs. 60,001 – Rs. 80,000
(e) Rs. 80,001 – Rs. 1,00,000
(f) Above Rs. 1,00,000

A.17 Annual income from this business

(a) Up to Rs. 20,000
(b) Rs. 20001 – Rs. 40,000
(c) Rs. 40001 – Rs. 60,000
(d) Rs. 60,001 – Rs. 80,000
(e) Rs. 80,001 – Rs. 1,00,000
(f) Above Rs. 1,00,000

(B) Motivational factors

B.1 Would you like your children to become entrepreneurs in the same occupation?

(a) Yes
(b) No

B.2 If No, give reasons:

(a) Children may not be interested
(b) This occupation is not profitable
(c) There is no future for this occupation
(d) Any other reason (Pl specify)

B.3 Are you willing to adapt new ideas for your business?

(a) Yes
(b) No
(c) Don't know

B.4 Please circle O the most appopriate responses for each statement

	Statement	*Strongly Diasgree*	*Disagree*	*Neither Agree nor Diasgree*	*Agree*	*Strongly Agree*
1.	I started this business to earn a livelihood	1	2	3	4	5
2.	I started this business to earn money	1	2	3	4	5
3.	I started this business to gain an independent living (self employment/be my own boss)	1	2	3	4	5
4.	I started this business to gain social prestige	1	2	3	4	5

(*Contd...*)

5.	I started this business to make use of idle funds	1	2	3	4	5
6.	I started this business because I was unemployed	1	2	3	4	5
7.	I started this business to diversify my economic interests.	1	2	3	4	5
8.	I started this business as I was influenced by the success stories of other entrepreneurs.	1	2	3	4	5
9.	I started this business because I enjoy the work.	1	2	3	4	5
10.	I started this business to give financial security to my family.	1	2	3	4	5

C. Impact of cluster on entrepreneurship development

C.1 Which of the following expectations stimulated your desire to take up sericulture

(a) Availability of land in the cluster

(b) Assistance from the state government or other agencies

(c) Availability of dug wells, bore wells, canals and ponds for irrigation

(d) Suitable climatic condition for silkworm rearing

(e) Availability of skilled labour for farming activities

(f) Any other reason (Pl specify)

C.2 Degree of fulfillment

(a) Very much fulfilled

(b) Fulfilled

(c) Undecided (neither fulfilled nor unfulfilled)

(d) Partly fulfilled

(e) Not at all fulfilled

C.3 Why did you choose this line of industry? Specify three reasons in the order of importance

(a) Easy to establish mulberry garden

(b) Ownership of agricultural land

(c) High margin of profit

(d) No difficulty in securing Disease-free-layings(Dfls)/seeds.

(e) No difficulty in securing rearing equiments/ appliances.

(f) Existence of similar units in the cluster

(g) Skill of farming/rearing

(h) Involvement of family labour

(i) Any other (Pl specify)

C.4 Why did you choose to locate your enterprise in the cluster? Specify three reasons in the order of importance.

(a) Availability of land in the cluster

(b) Availability of Dfls/seeds.

(c) Nearness to cocoon collection centre.

(d) Availability of transport facilities

(e) Existence of similar units in the cluster

(f) Government support and assistance

(g) Hometown or nearness to native place

(h) Suitable climatic condition

(i) Availabilty of rearing shed

(j) Any other reason (Pl specify)

C.5 Had there been no facility of cluster what might be your alternative proposals?

(a) Not to enter the same business

(b) To take up a job

(c) To set up the same business elsewhere

(d) To start a different business

(e) Can't say

C.6 Are you satisfied with common facilities available in the cluster?

(a) Very much satisfied

(b) Satisfied

(c) Undecided (neither satisfied nor dissatisfied)

(d) Not satisfied

(e) Not at all satisfied

Bibliography

Acharya, J. (1993). *Sericulture and development.* Indian Publishers Distributors, Delhi.

Acs, Z.J. (2006). How is entrepreneurship good for economic growth?. Innovations, 1(1), 97–107.

Agarwal, A.K. (1999). Industry in Mizoram, in A. Banerjee and B. Kar (eds), Ahmedabad, India.

Ahsan, M.M. (2000). Sericulture Status and Technologies for Cold and Temperate Conditions in India, Natl. Conf. Strat. Seric. Res. Dev. (Souvenir), 16-18 November 2000, CSR&TI, Mysore, 41-45.

Aldrich H (2000): Organizations evolving. Beverly Hills, Sage.

Aldridge, J.H. (1997). An Occupational Personality Profile of the Male entrepreneur as Assessed by the 16PF fifth edition, Unpublished doctoral dissertation, University of Georgia.

Amit, R., MacCrimmon, K.R., Zietsma, C., & Oesch, J.M. (2001). Does money matter: Wealth attainment as the motive for initiating growth-oriented technology ventures. *Journal of Business Venturing*, 16(2), 119–143.

Anna, V. (1990). Socio Economic Basis on Women Entrepreneurship. SEDME, 17(1), 17-47.

Awasthi, D. (2004). *Labour Process and Productivity in Micro and Small Enterprises (MSEs): the Indian Experience.* Paper presented at the 46th Annual Labour Economics Conference, organised by Institute of Development Studies, Jaipur. Bairwa, S.l., Lakra, K., Kushwaha, S., Meena, L.K., & Kumar, P. (2014).

Agripreneurship Development as a Tool to Upliftment of Agriculture. International Journal of Scientific and Research Publications, 4(3), 1-4.

Banerjee, A. (1994). Dairying systems in India. *Indian Dairyman, 46*, 229–234. Retrieved from https://ageconsearch.umn.edu/bitstream/58416/2/G-Srinivasa.pdf

Baruah, S.S. (2000). Women Entrepreneurs in North East- Role of Training in Creating and Sustaining Micro enterprises, in Prabath, S, V, V Patil, C Rani, R Shukla and Rao Gopala (eds). *Women Entrepreneurs in India: Challenges and Achievements*. NISIET, Indian Express Newspapers Ltd, Hyderabad.

Bass, B.M., & Stogdill, R.M. (1990). Bass & Stogdill's handbook of leadership: Theory, research, and managerial implications, New York: Free Press.

Baum, R. (1994). The Relation of Traits, Competencies, Vision, Motivation and Strategy to Venture Growth', unpublished doctoral dissertation, University of Maryland, College Park, MD.

Becattini, G. (1991). Italian Industrial Districts: Problem & Perspectives. *International Studies of Management and Organization*, 21(1), 83-90.

Benchamin, K. V., & Jolly, M. S. (1986). Principles of silkworm rearing. In S. Mahalingam (Ed.), *Proceedings of Seminar on Problems and Prospects of Sericulture* (pp. 63– 106). Central Sericultural Research & Training Institute, Mysore.

Berna, James, S.J. (1960). *Industrial Entrepreneurship in Madras State*, Asia Best, M. (1990). On the Clustering of Small Firms. *IDS Bulletin*, 23, 64-9.

Bewayo. & Edward, D. (1995). Uganda Entrepreneurs: Why they are in Business?, *Journal of Business Strategy*, 6(1), 67-78.

Bharathi, D. (2016). Sericulture Industry in India – A Source of Employment Generation. *International Journal of Advanced Engineering Research and Science* (IJAERS), 3(10), 144-147.

Bhat, T.A., & Choure, T. (2014). An economic analysis of mulberry raw silk production in traditional and non-traditional states of India. *World Journal of Economic and Finance,* 1(3), 016-020.

Bhola, R., Verheul, I., Grilo, I., & Thurik, A.R. (2006). Explaining engagement levels of opportunity and necessity entrepreneurs, Research report H200610. Zoetermeer: EIM Business and Policy Research.

Bhushi, U.M., & Pharsiyawar, S.M. (2004). Some perspectives in Silk and Powerloom Textile Industry- A Case Study. *International Engineering Management Conference.* Harvard University, Working paper, pp. 1-62.

Bird, B. (1988). Implementing entrepreneurial ideas: The case for intention. Academy of Management Review, 13(3), 442–453.

Breaugh, J.A. (1999). Further investigation of the work autonomy scales: Two studies.*Journal of Business and Psychology*, 13(3), 357–373.

Brusco, S. (1982). The Emilian Model: Productive Decentralisation and Social Integration. *Cambridge Journal of Economics*, 6, 167-84.

Burtner E Holly, and DP Moore (1997): Women's Organizational Exodus to Entrepreneurship: Self-reported Motivations and Correlates with Success, *Journal of Small Business Management*, 35, 1, 34-46.

Cantillon, R. (1755). *Essai sur la nature du commerce en general* (ed. H. Higgs) London: Macmillan (1931).

Carter, S. (1998). Portfolio entrepreneurship in the farm sector: Indigenous growth in rural area. *Entrepreneurship and Rural Development*, 10(1). 17-32.

Carter, N.M., Gartner, W.B., Shaver, K.G., & Gatewood, E.J. (2003). The career reasons of nascent entrepreneurs. *Journal of Business Venturing*, 18(1), 13–39.

Cassar, G. (2007). Money, money, money? A longitudinal investigation of entrepreneur career reasons, growth preferences and achieved growth. *Entrepreneurship and Regional Development*, 19(1), 89–107.

Cawthorne, P. (1995). Of Networks and Markets: The Rise and Rise of a South Indian Town, the Example of Tiruppur's Cotton Knitwear Industry. *World Development*, 23(1).

Central Silk Board. (2012). *Functioning of Central Silk Board and Performance of Indian Silk Industry.* Central Silk Board, Ministry of Textiles, Govt. of India.

Retrieved from http://texmin.nic.in/sites/default/files/note-on-sericulture-EnglishOct2018.pdf.

Central Silk Board. (2015). Intensive Bivoltine Sericulture Technology Package, Central Sericultural Research & Training Institure (IS0 9001: 2015 Certified), Govt. of India: Ministry of Textiles, West Bengal.

Central Silk Board. (2018). Retrieved from http://csb.gov.in/silk-sericulture/sericulture/.

Central Silk Board. (2019). *Functioning of Central Silk Board and Performance of Indian Silk Industry*. Central Silk Board, Ministry of Textiles, Govt. of India. Retrieved from http://texmin.nic.in/sites/default/files/note-on-sericulture-EnglishOct2018.pdf.

Census of India. (2011). Retrieved from: http://www.censusindia.gov.in/2011Census/pes/Pesreport.pdf

Chandan, R., Mukherjee, R., & Ghosh, S. (2013). Sericulture as an Employment Generating Household Industry in West Bengal - A Study on its Current Problems & Prospects, MPRA Paper No. 43672, posted 9. January 2013. Retrieved from https://mpra.ub.uni-muenchen.de/43672/.

Chandrashekar, R.T. (1987) Income and Employment generation in Sericulture via-vis alternative crops in Hosur Taluk in Dharmapuri District Univertsity ofAgricultural Sciences, Bangalore 1987.

Chandrashekar, R.R. (1990). Inome and employment genmeration in Sericulture Via-vis alternative crops in Hosut Taluk in Dharmapuri Distirct. University of Agricultural Sciences, Bangalore 1990, Page no. 128.

Chhetri, K. (2018). *Impact of cluster processes on entrepreneurship development: A study of Daramdin Rose Cluster, Sikkim* (Unpublished master's thesis). Aizawl: Department of Commerce, Mizoram University.

Cho, M.R. (1994). Weaving Flexibility: Large–Small Firm Relations, Flexibility and Regional Clusters in South Korea, in P.O. Pedersen, A. Sverisson and. van Dijk, M, P (Eds), F*lexible Specialization: The Dynamics of Small-scale Industry in the South*, London: Intermediate Technology, London.

Choudhury, B.N., Engzananga, D., Vanlallawma, C., Pachuau, L., Deori, S., & Biswas, T.K. (2013). Development of Sericulture in Mizoram: An alternative source of livelihood for the Tribal Communities. Souvenir and compendium, 1st Bodoland National Seminar-cum-workshop on Sericulture industry and its role in the socioEconomic Upliftment in Rural Society, 10-11 August 2013, pp 139-145.

Choudhury, B.N., Das, S.C., & Ahmed M. (2017). Studies on Knowledge and Adoption Level of Sericultural Technologies among the Farmers of Aizawl District of Mizoram. *Imperial Journal of Interdisciplinary Research,* 3(5), 1573-1578.

Cole, A. (1959). *Business Enterprise in Social Setting,* Cambridge, Mass., Harvard University Press, 1959.

Chowdhuri, R.S., Umasankar., Das, N.K,, Sahu, P.K., Majumdar, M.K. (2011). Studies on involvement of women and their contribution share in sericulture activities. *Journal of Crop and Weed*, 7(2), 37-40.

Christiansen, C. (1997). *The Innovators Dilemma*, Harvard Business School Press. CSRTI. (2005). Disinfection and Hygiene in Silkworm Rearing, Central

Sericultural Research & Training Institute (ISO 9001: 2015 Certified), Central Silk Board, Ministry of Textiles, Govt. of India, Srirampura.

Cuervo, A., Ribeiro, D., & Roig, S. (2005). *Entrepreneurship: concepts, theory and perspective.* Retrieved from http://www.uv.es/bcjauveg/docs/LibroCuervo RibeiroRoigIntroduction.pdf.

Das, B. (2000). Emerging Trends In Women Entrepreneurship: A Study Of Kamrup District Of Assam, in Prabath, S, V; Patil V,C Rani, Shukla ,R; Rao Gopala;(eds). *Women Entrepreneurs in India: Challenges and Achievements*, NISIET, Indian Express Newspapers Ltd, Hyderabad, pp 172-186.

Das, K. (1995). Industrial Clustering in Developing Countries. *Productivity (Special Issue on Small Scale Sector)*, 36(1).

Das, K. (1999). Flexibility, Collectivity and Labour: Contextualizing the Industrial Cluster Debate in India. *The Indian Journal of Labour Economics.*

Das, K. (2003). *Competition and Response in Small Firm Clusters: Two Cases from Western India*, Gujarat Institute of Development Research, Ahmedabad, India, working paper no.142.

Das, K. (2005). *Industrial clusters in India: Perspectives and Issues for Research*, Working Paper No. 159, Gujarat Institute of Development Research, Gota, Differences between Entrepreneurs and Managers", *Journal of Small Business Management*, Vol. 47, No. 4, pp. 401-421.

Datta, R. K. (1992). *Guidelines for bivoltine rearing*. Bangalore: Central Silk Board.

Das, R., & Das, K. (2011). Industrial cluster: An approach for rural development in North East India. International *Journal of Trade, Economics and Finance,* 2(2), 15-32.

Deshingkar, P., & Farrington J. (2006). Rural labour markets in South Asia: Evidence from India and Bangladesh. *World Development Report.*

Dewangan, S.K. (2017). Sericulture play key role to employment generation and socio- economic empowerment of tribal women", *International Journal of Advanced Research and Development*, 2(6), 761-768.

Directorate of Economics and Statistics. (2012). *Statistical handbook*, Mizoram, Directorate of Economics and Statistics, Government of Mizoram.

Directorate of Sericulture: Aizawl, Mizoram. (2012). *Sericulture at a glance*, Information and Publicity Cell, Government of Mizoram.

Diana, M.H., Maija, R., & Charles, H.M. (2012). The nascent entrepreneurship hub: goals, entrepreneurial self-efficacy and start-up outcomes.

Dollinger, M.J. (1995). Entrepreneurship Strategies and Resources, Irwin, Homewood.

Drucker, P.F. (1985). *Innovation and Entrepreneurship*, Oxford: Butterworth Heinemann, 1985.

Elwee, G. (2007). Important trends and required skills in England (UK). In Pieter de Wolf and Schoorleemer (Ed.). Exploring the Significance of Entrepreneurship in Agriculture, FiBL Publishers, and Switzerland, (2007), 18-28.

Eswarappa, K. (2011). Development initiatives and sericulture in a south Indian village. *South Asia Research*, *31*(3), 213–229.

Eswarappa, K. (2013). Role of women in sericulture and community development: A study from a south Indian village. *SAGE Open*. Retrieved from http://sgo.sagepub.com/content/3/3/2158244013502984.

Feldman, D.C., & Bolino, M.C. (2000). Career patterns of the self-employed: Career motivations and career outcomes. *Journal of Small Business Management*, 38(1), 53–67.

Foundation for MSME Clusters. (2007). Policy and Status Paper on Cluster Development in India. Retrieved from www.msmefoudation.org.

Foundation for MSME Clusters. (2009). Clustering for Progress: The Road Traveled and The Way Ahead. Retrieved from www.msmefoundation.org.

Gaikwad, V.R., & Tripathi, R.N. (1970). *Socio- Psychological Factors Influencing Industrial entrepreneurship in Rural Areas,* National Institute of Community Development, Hyderabad.

Gangadhara, R.N. (1986). *Entrepreneurship and Growth of Enterprises in Industrial Estates*, Deep and Deep Publications Pvt. Ltd, New Delhi.

Garg, R.B.L. (1979). Sericulture industry- The challenges ahead. Agricultural banker, 11(4), 7-10.

Government of India. (2013). *Annual Report 2012-13*, Central Silk Board, Ministry of Textiles, Government of India, Bangalore.

Government of Karnataka. (2011). *Integrated agribusiness development policy*, Department of agriculture, Government of Karnataka, Bangalore.

Government of Mizoram. (2011). *Mizoram Remote Sensing Application Centre (MIRSAC)*, Science & Technology, Planning Department, Government of Mizoram.

Government of Mizoram. (2012). *Sericulture at a glance, information and publicity cell*. Aizawl: Directorate of Sericulture.

Government of Mizoram. (2014). *Economic Survey, 2013–14*. Planning & Programme Implementation Department.

Gray, C. (2002). Entrepreneurship, resistance to change and growth in small firms. *Journal of Small Business and Enterprises Development*, 9(1), 61-72.

Grilo, I., & Thurik A R (2006), “Entrepreneurship in the old and new Europe. In E. Santarelli (Ed.), Entrepreneurship, growth, and innovation: The dynamics of firms and industries: International studies in entrepreneurship”, Berlin: Springer Science, pp. 75–103.

Hanumappa, H.G., & Erappa, S. (1985). Economic issues in sericulture: study of Karnataka. *Economic and Political Weekly* 20(31), 3122-3224.

Hazare, T. N. & Jadav. (2008). Sericulture Brings Better Income. *Indian Silk,* 46 (9)

Hessels, J., Gelderen, M.V., & Thurik, R. (2008). Entrepreneurial aspirations, motivations and drivers. Small Business Econ, Vol. 31, Sept. 2008, 323-339.

Hessels, J., Van, G.M., & Thurik, R. (2008). Drivers of entrepreneurial aspirations at the country level: the role of start-up motivations and social security. *International Entrepreneurship and Management Journal, forthcoming.*

Higgins, R. (1998). Local Business Co-operation, Training and Enterprise Councils: The Development of Inter-firm Networks. *Regional Studies*, 32(9), 813-826.

Hisrich, R.D. (1985). The Woman Entrepreneur in the United States and Puerto Rico: a Comparative Study. *Leadership and Organizational Development Journal*, Vol. 5, 3–8.

Holmstrom, M.M. (1993). A New Direction for Indian Industry? Bangalore as an Industrial District, *Report to the Overseas Development Administration*, School of Development Studies, University of East Anglia, Norwich, mimeo.

Hornaday, J., & Aboud, J. (1973). Characteristics of Successful Entrepreneurs. *Personnel Psychology,* 24, 141–153.

House, R.J., & Shamir, B. (1993). Toward the integration of transformational, charismatic and visionary theories of leadership, In M. Chemers & R. Ayman (Eds.). *Leadership theory and research: Perspectives and directions*, San Diego, CA: Academic Press, 81–107.

Hundal, P.S. (1977). *Entrepreneurial Motivation and its Structure*, ICSSR, New Delhi.

Indian Institute of Entrepreneurship. (2005). *Evaluation cum Impact Study of STEP Project for Handloom Weavers of Assa'*, Indian Institute of Entrepreneurship, Guwahati.

Jagannathan, N. (1995). Impacts of sericulture on income and employment generation. *Indian Silk*, 33, 11-16.

Kabra, K.C. (2008). *Economic Growth of Mizoram- Role of Business and Industry*, Concept Publishing House, New Delhi.

Kannan, V.A. (1987). Women in Silk industry. *Indian Silk*, 26(5), 4-7.

Kashyap. S.P. (1992). *Recent Developments in the Small Enterprises Sector in India: Economic and Social Aspects'*, Discussion Paper No. 48, International Institute of Labour Studies, ILO, Geneva.

Kasi, E. (2013). Role of women in sericulture and community development: A study from a south Indian village. *SAGE*, 3(3), 1-11. Retrieved from http://sgo.sagepub.com/content /3/3/2158244013502984.

Khanka, S.S. (1990). *Entrepreneurship in Small-Scale Industries*, Himalaya Publishing, New Delhi.

Khanka, S.S. (2009). Motivational Orientation of Assamese Entrepreneurs in the SME Sector, *Journal of Entrepreneurship*, 18(2), 209-218.

Knight, F.H. (1942). Profit and Entrepreneurial Functions. *The Tasks of Common History: Supplement to Journal of Economic History*, 2, 126-132.

Knorringa, P. (1998). Barriers to Flexible Specialization in Agra's Footwear Industry, in M. Holmstrom,M and P. Cadene (eds). *Decentralized Production in India, Industrial Districts, Flexible Specialization and Employment*, Sage Publications, 283–307, New Delhi.

Kolvereid, L. (1992). Growth aspirations among Norwegian entrepreneurs. *Journal of Business Venturing*, 7(3), 209–222.

Kolvereid, L. (1996). Organizational employment versus self-employment: Reasons for career choice intentions. *Entrepreneurship Theory and Practice*, 20(3), 23–31.

Krishnaswami, S., Narasimhanna, S., Suryananrayana, S. K., & Kumarararaj, S. (1973). *Silkworm rearing:Sericulture Mannual-2*. Agricultural Services Bulletin. 15/2, FAO. Rome: United Nations Organization.

Krishnaswami, D.N.S. (1986). Mulberry Cultivation in South India. Central Sericultural Research & Training lnstitute, Mysore, Published by: Shri V. Balasubramanian, lAS, Member-SecretarY Central Silk Board United Mansions No. 39, Bangalore

Kumara, S.B.K.(1993). Mulberry for drylands of Karnataka. Indian Silk Central Silk Board, Bangalore 1992.XXXI (6), 5-10.

Lakshmanan, S., & Jayram, H. (1998). Manpower utilization in mulberry sericulture: An empirical analysis. Manpower Journal, 33, 49-63.

Lakhshmanan, S., & Geetha, D. (2007). Tamil Nadu—Employment Opportunities in Sericulture.*Indian Silk*, *46*(7):18–20.

Lakshmanan, S., Mallikarjuna, B., Ganapathy, R. R., Jayaram, H., & Geetha, D. R. G. (1998). Studies on adoption of sericultural innovations at farmer's field in Tamil Nadu: An empirical analysis. *Indian Journal of Sericulture*, *37*(1), 52–56.

Laskar, B.I. (2010). *Industrialisation in Mizoram-Problems and Prospects*, NCBA, Delhi.

Lianzela. (1994*). Economic Development of Mizoram*, Spectrum Publications, Guwahati.

Locke, E.A., & Latham, G. (1990). A theory of goal setting and task performance, Englewood Cliffs, New Jersey: Prentice Hall.

Locke, E.A. (2000). *The prime movers.* New York: Amacom.

Locke, E.A., & Baum, J.R. (2007). Entrepreneurial motivation. In J. R. Baum, M. Frese, & R. A. Baron (Eds.), The psychology of entrepreneurship, Mahwah, NJ: Erlbaum, 93–112.

Mahesha, H.B.Dr. (2008). Life Cycle of Bombyx mori, Mysore. Retrieved From: http://hbmahesh.weebly.com/uploads/3/4/2/2/3422804/3.life_cyclemorphology_of_b._mori-o_e_word_13-14.pdf

Mali, D.D. (2000). Women Entrepreneurs In North-East India- A Few Cases of Created Entrepreneurs, in Prabath, S, V, V Patil ,C Rani, R Shukla and Rao Gopala (eds), *Women Entrepreneurs in India: Challenges and Achievement*s, NISIET, Indian Express Newspapers Ltd, Hyderabad, 89-97.

Manimala, J.M. (1999). *Entrepreneurial Policies and Strategies: the Innovator's Choice*, Sage Publications.

Manimala, M.J., Mitra, J., Singh, V. (2009). Enterprise support system: Nature and relevance. In Mathew J. Manimala, J. Mitra & V. Singh (Eds.), *Enterprise support system: An international perspective* (pp. 1–35). New Delhi: Response Books.

Markley, D., & Macke, D. (2003). Entrepreneurial support organizations. *The Centre for Rural Entrepreneurship*, Monograph, 6: 1–4.

Marshall, A. (1907). Principles of Economics, Macmillan, London.

Marshall, A. (1919). *Industry and Trade*, Macmillan, London Publishers, New Delhi.

Maslow, A.H. (1954). Motivation and Personality, New York: Harper & Row.

McClelland, D.C. (1961). The achieving society, Princeton:Van Nostrand.

McClelland, D.C., & David, H.B. (1976). *Power is the Great Motivator*, Harvard Business Review Classics, HBR.

Mills, K. G., Reynolds, E. B., & Reamer, A. (2008). *Clusters and competitiveness: A new federal role for stimulating regional economies*. Washington, DC: Brookings Institution Metropolitan Policy Programme.

Mishra, P. (2000). Women Entrepreneurs: are They Enterprising and Empowered Enough? - A Study in Small Scale Industrial sector of Orissa, in Prabath, S, V, V Patil, C Rani, R Shukla and Rao Gopala, (eds), *Women Entrepreneurs in India: Challenges and Achievements*, NISIET, Indian Express Newspapers Ltd, Hyderabad, pp 142-154.

Mitsui, I. (2003). Industrial Cluster Policies and Regional Development in the age of Globalisation – Eastern and Western approaches and their Differences, presented in 30th International Small Business Congresses, 22nd September, 2003.

Mittal R. (2006). Entrepreneurship development through agripreneurship in India: Crossing the boundaries with Agri-Export Zones (AEZ) National Institute of Agricultural Marketing, Agribusiness & Entrepreneurship Cell.

Morris, M.H., Miyasaki, N.N., Watters, C.E., & Coombes, S.M. (2006). The dilemma of growth: Understanding venture size choices of women entrepreneurs. *Journal of Small Business Management,* 44(2), 221–244.

Murthy. (1978). Sericulture can generate employment" Indian Silk, Central Silk Board, Bangalore. 1978 vol. 28, Page no. 36.

Nadvi, K. (1995). The Export Competitiveness of Small Producers: the Surgical Instruments Cluster of Sialkot'. Pakistan, mimeo, Brighton: *Institute of Development Studies*, University of Sussex

Nadvi, K., & Barrientos, S. (2004). *Industrial Clusters and Poverty Reduction: towards a Methodology for Poverty Reduction and Social Impact Assessment of Cluster Development Initiatives,* UNIDO, Vienna. Retrieved from http://www.ids.ac.uk/ids/global/pdfs/SB&KN_UNIDO2004.pdf

Nafziger, E., & Wayne. (1978). *Class, Caste and Entrepreneurship: A Study of Indian Industrialists*. The University Press of Hawaii, Honolulu.

Nagalakshmi, T., & Sudhakar, A. (2013). A case study of Dharmapuri farmers. International Journal of Science and Research, 2 (8), 208-214.

Naidu, E.M., & Naidu, B.J. (1984) Sericulture and Rural development in 7th plan, Southern Economist 1984, 23 (2), 23-25.

Narasaiah, M.L. (2003). Problems and prospects of sericulture. Discovery Publishing House, New Delhi.

Narasaiah, P.V., Rathnam, N.V., & Murthy, S.D. (2013). Current Status of Silk Industry in India- An Evaluation. Small Enterprises Development, Management & Extension (SEDME), 40(4).

Narendran, K., & Ranganathan, T.T. (2015). Agripreneurship for Rural Youth. International Journal in Management and Social Science, 3(8), 245-251.

NCEUS. (2009). Retrieved from: www.nceus.gov.in

OECD. (2007). *Reviews of Regional Innovation, Competitive Regional Clusters, National policy Approaches*, OECD.

Ollenburg, C., & Buckley, R. (2007). Stated Economic and Social Motivations of Farm Tourism Operators. *Journal of Travel Research*, SAGE Publications, 45(4), 445447.

Ostwald, M., Jonsson, A., Wibeck, V., & Asplund, T. (2012). Mapping energy crop cultivation and identifying motivational factors among Swedish farmers, *Biomass & Bioenergy,* 50, 25-34.

Pal, S., & K, Sood. (2004). *Dynamics of Growth and Stagnation of Industrial Clusters in India: Emerging Issues and Policy Imperatives'*, Entrepreneurship Development Institute of India, Ahmedabad.

Panday, P.N., Sharan S.K., & Mishra, P.K. (2005). *A biochemical approach: Silk culture*. APH Publishing Corporation, New Delhi.

Parilli, M.D. (2007). Cluster Trajectories in Developing Countries: A Stage and Eclectic Approach Applied to Survival Clusters in Central America', in Pitelis, C; Sugden, R and Wilson, J, R (Eds), *Clusters and Globalisation: The Development of Urban and Regional Economies*, Edward Elgar, USA.

Piore, M.J., & Sabel, C.F. (1984). *The Second Industrial Divide - Possibilities for Prosperity*. USA: Basic Books.

Porter, M. (1990). *The Competitive Advantage of Nations*. London: Macmillan.

Porter, M. (1998). *On Competition*, Harvard Business Review Book. Publishing House, Bombay.

Porter, M. (1998). Clusters and the New Economics of Competition. *Harvard Business Review*, 76(6), 77–91.

Porter, M. E. (1998). Clusters and the new economics of competition. *Harvard Business Review*, *76*(6), 77–91. Retrieved from http://www.alanausterman.com/wpcontent/uploads/2009/12/Clusters-The-New-Economics-of-CompetitionMichael-Porter.pdf

Porter, M. (1998). On Competition: New Agendas for Companies, Governments and Institutions, Harvard Business School Press, Boston

Priyadarshini, M.B., & Kumari, N.V. (2013). A Study on the knowledge and adoption level of improved sericulture practices by the farmers of Chittoor district. *International Journal of Agricultural Science and Research*, 3(2), 43-46.

Prakasam, K., & Ravi, G. Dr. (2014). Sericulture-An Ideal Enterprise for Sustainable Income in Erode District of Tamil Nadu. *Language in India*, ISSN 1930-2940, Vol. 14, No.9.

Puera, J., P, Siiskonen., & Vesala K.M. (2012). Entrepreneurial identity among the rural small business owner managers in Finland: In rurality, rural policy and politics in Nordic-Scottish perspective, HW Tanvig (ed). Esbjerg: Danish Centre for Rural Research and Development. Working Paper 1/2012.

Ragjagopalan. (1980). Impact of sericulture on income and employment in rural areas in TamilNadu. *Indian Silk*, Central Silk Board, XVI (7), 7-15.

Rahmathulla, V.K., & Geethadevi, R.G. (2000). Sericulture – An apt venture for rural betterment, *Agriculture Today*, 3(4), 46-48.

Rahmathulla,V.K. (2012). Management of Climatic Factors for Successful Silkworm(Bombyx mori L.) Crop and Higher Silk Production: A Review. *Hindawi Publishing Corporation, Psyche*. Retreieved from https://www.hindawi.com/journals/psyche/2012/121234/

Rajapurohit, A.R., & Govindaraju, K.V. (1981). Employment and Income in Sericulture. *Shiny Publications*, Bangalore 1981. Page no. 225.

Ramakrishna, N., & Reddy, D.N.R. (1995). Sericulture – A Role Model for Self employment. Farmer & Parliament, September: 19-20.

Ramarao. (1978). Employement potential of Sericulture Industry. *Indian Silk*, Central Silk Board, Bangalore. 1978, 17 (6), 67-71.

Ramswamy, R., & Kumar, J. N. V. R. (2011). Impact of cluster on entrepreneurship in tribal artisan clusters: A case study of Thenzawl handloom cluster, Mizoram. *SEDME*, *38*(2), 39–51.

Ramswamy, R., & Kumar J.N.V.R. (2012). Motivational Factors of Tribal Entrepreneurs in Handloom Clusters: A Case Study of Thenzawl, Mizoram. *IUP Journal of Entrepreneurship Development*, 9(4), 56-68.

Rathnam, N. V., & Narasaiah, P. V. (2012). Sericulture industry—A boon for rural poor: Special focus on Chittoor District of A.P. *SEDME*, *39*(3), 17–33.

Raymond, W., & Habiyaremye, A. (2013). *Sericulture on thousand hills: Reeling Rwanda out of poverty*. Retrieved from file:///C:/Users/Examxx/Downloads/Raymond_Habiyaremye%20(1).pdf Rocha, H. O. (2004). Entrepreneurship and development: The role of clusters. *Small Business Economics*, *23*(5), 363–400.

Rani, G.S. (2006). Women in Sericulture, ISBN 81-81-8356-098-9, Discovery Publishing House, New Delhi.

Rathnam, N.V., & Narasaiah, P.V. (2012). Sericulture Industry – A Boon for Rural Poor: Special Focus on Chittoor District of A.P. *SEDME* 39(3), 17-33.

Rathnam, N.V., & Narasaiah, P.V. (2012). Sericulture Industry – A Boon for Rural Poor: Special Focus on Chittoor District of A.P. *SEDME* 39(3), 17-33.

Rathnam, N., Narasaiah, P.V., & Murthy, S.D. (2013). Current status of silk industry in India – An evaluation. *SEDME*, 40(4), 55-67.

Raymond, W., & Habiyaremye, A. (2013*)*. Sericulture on thousand Hills: Reeling Rwanda out of poverty. Retrieved from www.merit.unu.edu/MEIDE/papers/2013/Raymond_Habiyaremye.pdf.

Reynolds, P.D., Camp, S.M., Bygrave, W.D., Autio, E., & Hay, M. (2001). Global Entrepreneurship Monitor: 2001 Executive Report, Kansas City, MO: Kauffman Center for Entrepreneurial Leadership.

Rocha, H., & R, Sternberg. (2005). Entrepreneurship: The Role of Clusters Theoretical Perspectives and Empirical Evidence from Germany, *Small Business Economics*, 24, 3(02), 267-292.

Rodi, L. (2013). Unpublished MPhil Thesis "Entrepreneurship among street vendors of vegetables in Aizawl, Mizoram, (MPhil Thesis, Department of Commerce, Mizoram University).

Rosenfeld, S. (1997). Bringing Business Clusters into the Mainstream of Economic Development. *European Planning Studies*, 5, 3–23.

Rotter, J.B. (1966). Generalized expectancies for internal versus external control of reinforcement. Psychological Monographs: General and Applied, 80, 609.

Roy, C., Mukherjee, S., & Ghosh, S. (2012). *Sericulture as an employment generating household industry in West Bengal: A study on its current problems & prospects*. Munich Personal RePEc Archive Paper No. 43672. Retrieved from https://mpra.ub.uni-muenchen.de/43672/

Roy, P., & Sarkar, R. (2015). Work participation and income generation from sericulture: A case study of Alomtola village of Kaliachak-II block in Malda district, West Bengal. *Social and Economic Geography*, *1*(1), 31–36.

Sastry, D. U. (1984), op.cit., pp. 89-92.

Sathish, A.V. (1985). Infact of Diversification and Liberal Credit Policy on Income and Employment of Non-Viable farmers in Pithepuram block of East Godavari Dist (A.P.). *Indian Journal of Agricultural Economics,* 1985 XL, (3), 323-329.

Sati, V.P. (2008). Natural Resource Management and Food Security in the Alaknanda Basin of Garhwal Himalaya. *ENVIS Bulletin: Himalayan Ecology*, 16(2), 1–11.

Say, J.B. (1803). *A Treatise on Political Economy: or, the Production, Distribution and Consumption of Wealth*, New York: Augustus M. Kelley (1964).

Singh, A.P. (2012). Strategies for developing agripreneurship among farming community in Uttar Pradesh. *Journal of Asia Entrepreneurship and Sustainability,* 8(1), 81102.

Singh, T. (2012). Sericulture, Applied Zoology. Retrieved from http://www.gonder.org.tr/wp-content/uploads/2016/04/sericulture-silkwormgenel-bilgi.pdf.

Shane, S., Kolvereid, L., & Westhead, P. (1991). An exploratory examination of the reasons leading to new firm formation across country and gender. *Journal of Business Venturing*, 6(6), 431–446.

Shane, S., Locke, E.A., & Collins, C.J. (2003). Entrepreneurial motivation. Human Resource Management, Review 13, 257–279.

Sharma, K.L. (1975). *Entrepreneurial Performance in Role Perspective*, Abhinav Publications, New Delhi.

Schmitz, H. (1995). Small Shoemakers and Fordist Giants: Tale of a Super cluster. *World Development*, 23(1), 9–28.

Schumpeter, J. (1934). *The theory of economic development*, Harvard University Press.

Srinivasa, G., Kumaresan, P., & Vijayaprakash, N.B. (2008). Economic analysis of resource use efficiency in sericulture. *Indian Journal of Sericulture*. 47(1), 29-33.

Srivastav, N., & Raj, S. (2007). Marketing Management and Entrepreneurship Development in a Tribal Dominated Economy: A Case Study of Small Scale Industries in East Khasi Hills District of Meghalaya. *The ICFAI Journal of Entrepreneurship Development*, Vol. No. 4, 28-47, December 28-47.

Thiripura K and Ramalakshmi P, (2018), "Silk Production: The Global Scenerio", Asian Review of Social Sciences, Vol. 7, No. 2, pp. 22-24.

Thurik, A.R., Carreer, M.A., Van, S.A.J., & Audretsch, D.B. (2008). Does self-employment reduce unemployment?, *Journal of Business Venturing, forthcoming*.

Timmons, J.A. (2000). New venture creation: Entrepreneurship (5th ed.). Homewood, IL: Irwin.

Townsend, S. (2013) He will not be beet-en: Farmer fights back at cheap imports. The Telegraph, 06/06/2013, p. 14. Retrieved from: https://epubs.scu.edu.au/cgi/viewcontent.cgi?article=1615&context=theses

Tripathi, R., & Agarwal, S. (2015). Rural development through agripreneurship: a study of farmers in Uttar Pradesh. *Global Journal of Advanced Research*, 2(2), 534-542.

Trivedi, S., & Sarkar, K. (2015). Comparative study on income generation through agriculture crop and sericulture at farmer's level in Murshidabad district. *Journal of Entomology and Zoology Studies*, 3(1), 242-245.

Udeda, S., Kimura, R., & Suzuki, K. (1975). Studies on the growth of the silkworm Bombyx mori. IV mutual relationship between the growth in the fifth instar larvae and productivity of silk substance and eggs. *Bulletin of the Sericultural Experiment Station*, *26*(3), 233–247.

Umesh, K.B., Akshara, M., Shripad, B., Harish, Kumar., & Srinivasan, S.M.(2009). Performance Analysis of Production and Trade of Indian Silk under WTO Regime. Contributed Paper prepared for presentation at the International Association of Agricultural Economists Conference, Beijing, China, August 16-22, 2009

UNIDO. (2001). Women Entrepreneurship Development in Selected African Countries, Working Paper No.7.

Van, G.M.W., & Jansen, P.G.W. (2006). Autonomy as a startup motive. *Journal of Small Business and Enterprise Development*, 13(1), 23–32.

Verghese, G., & Thanzawna, R.L. (1997). *A History of the Mizos Volume –I*, Vikas, New Delhi.

Vishakanta. (2018). Cost and Benefits of Sericulture Farmers of Ramanagaram District of Karnataka. *International Journal for Research in Applied Science & Engineering Technology*, 6(4).

Wayne, H., Stewart, Jr., & Philip, L. R. (2007). A Meta_ Analysis of Achievement Motivation. *The Journal of Entrepreneurship*, 18(2), 209–218.

Wennekers, S., Van, S.A., Thurik, R., & Reynolds, P. (2005). Nascent entrepreneurship and the level of economic development. *Small Business Economics*, 24(3), 293–309.

Wilson, F., Marlino, D., & Kickul, J. (2004). Our entrepreneurial future: Examining the diverse attitudes and motivations of teens across gender and ethnic identity. *Journal of Developmental Entrepreneurship*, 9(3), 177–197.

Yadaiah & Sarangapani. (1994). Economics of sericulture – A micro level study, Agri banker, 17(1), 38-40.

Index

D

E

F

G

H

T

U

V

W

Y

Z

जान जा
जीवन जीने की कला